I Just Want to be Happy Again

"How to Find Yourself Again When Facing Life Struggles"

By Beth Elkassih

ISBN: 978-1-7368363-0-9

Printed in USA

DEDICATION

To My Mother – A strong and gentle soul who taught me to believe in God, believe in hard work and always be kind and respectful to all. I humbly aspire to be like her!

To Anyone Suffering From Depression, etc. – For those of you who are currently suffering from depression, anxiety, sadness or grief, this book was written to you for sincere encouragement, inspiration and assurance that 'this too shall pass' and you WILL reclaim your happiness, you WILL find yourself again and you will come through to the other side. KNOW that you are both unique and special and deserve to be happy.

ACKNOWLEDGEMENTS

I first give thanks to God for guiding me in creating and preparing this much-needed message to share with others, especially those who are currently suffering from depression, anxiety, sadness, grief and other mental health illnesses. God has blessed me with the gift of writing and I feel it is my duty to convey both important and vital messages of hope to all.

I want to give the greatest of gratitude for the love and support of my immediate family – my husband Abed, and daughters, Patty, Layla and Nadean.

I have been blessed with many family and friends, both whom I've known all my life and those who I've met recently. My sincere thanks to Brittany Ballard, Carolyn Howard, Jan Cook, Mary Johnson, Poovanesh Pather, Mernell King, Elaine Bowen-Platz, Gayle Wilt, Patty Luu, Ellen Ravkind, Michelle Sillery, Ava Mills, Theresa Jarboe, Stasia Anderson, Marlette Jarboe, Ben Jarboe, Elizabeth Foti, Andrea Hyde and to Haley Gray.

I am really fortunate to have Muhammad Umair Qureshi, creator of www.zulzan.com, cross my life path and journey beginning in October 2018. He has not only been the best web developer I've ever worked with, but his inspiration and humble guidance to encourage me to use the gift of writing that God blessed me with does not go unnoticed. I will be eternally grateful for his loyalty and support. He is not only my business associate but a true friend.
Thank you Umair.

For more information:

www.zulzan.com, www.wpstairs.com & www.snapybiz.com

Table of Contents

Table of Contents

Introduction

You and I know all too well no one can be happy 'all the time'. No one is immune from suffering from depression, sadness, anxiety, etc. from time to time.

Let me ask you a question. When you DO experience these days or moments', what do you do? Wouldn't it be nice to be able to just tap into a place where someone actually cares? Where your feelings are heard and where you can find empathy and support to help you get through that moment?

As a survivor of acute post-partum depression, several bouts of clinical depression and one who currently deals with anxiety from time to time, I wanted to create a platform to help as many silent 'sufferers' with answering the all too familiar cry: "I just want to be happy again!"

This book is a collection of 14 of the most popular blog posts from 'Made You Smile Back', a professional blog dedicated in providing daily encouragement, inspiration and thought-provoking content for everyone facing everyday life struggles.

But most importantly, **'I Just Want to be Happy Again'** was written to be provide hope and be another 'go-to' resource to those who simply just want to be heard. Let me help you regain your happiness, and to find yourself again while facing these life struggles. You DESERVE to be happy again.

"Turn Your Tears of Sadness Into Tears of Happiness"
- Umair Qureshi

CHAPTER ONE
WHY CAN'T I BE HAPPY AGAIN!

Why can't I just be happy again was written to reach out to anyone and everyone who is looking for encouragement and how to come back to themselves and be the happy, positive and productive person they were in the past.

Why can't I be happy is a familiar cry from many in the world today. We all want to experience joy again. If you're suffering from acute depression, anxiety, or perhaps being a new mother experiencing the baby blues, or who are in the throes of post-partum depression, we all just want to be happy again.

Are you tired of being sad? Perhaps you don't even know why you're sad. Get back to your 'happy place'. This chapter is meant for you!

Life isn't about waiting for the storm to pass...
It's learning to dance in the rain.
- Unknown

HOW DO I STOP BEING SO UNHAPPY?

"Why can't I just be happy?" Wouldn't it be nice if we could just go back in time and experience that one childhood moment when we experienced happiness as a state of being — of feeling inexplicable joy?

That one incredible moment when everything in our world was perfect, inside and out. Why can't I just be this happy again!

In this chapter, I am going to discuss various reasons as to why we feel this way from time to time. We will also look at innovative ways of how you can stop being so unhappy and how we can overcome this temporary 'state of being' and find our happiness again.

I'M JUST SO TIRED OF FEELING THIS WAY!

Do you know why you're not happy? Have you caught yourself thinking that all the things that used to make you *happy* aren't making you *happy* any longer? Sometimes the reason you can't be happy is not that complicated.

All one has to do is just step out of yourself for a moment and ask your psyche why you're so unhappy. You may be in a difficult situation and you see no way out.

Or things that once brought you joy, have lost their sparkle. This isn't your fault. You may be stuck in an emotional rut.

You know you want to be happy. You wouldn't be reaching out if you didn't. And there my friend lies the power that is truly within you to change things around!

If you set your sights on all the right targets and/or goals and get your priorities straight, you can become *happy again.*

CAN YOU FORCE YOURSELF TO BE HAPPY?

You're stronger than you realize and you have the power within you to *choose* to do whatever it takes to **Make You Smile Again.**

You should never force feelings or emotions upon yourself. ... However, you can "trick" your brain into feeling happy by doing things like smiling and engaging in things that you love

YOU'RE NOT ALONE...

For myself, I strive to spend the majority of my day *smiling* at others with the intent of making those I meet feel good about themselves. I even read somewhere that even with the act of *smiling* itself, it does seem to help. Something about the feel-good neurotransmitters being released. But I digress.

Here's the deal. Maybe your unhappiness is a type of *depression*. Would it surprise you to know that depression is a medical condition and is considered a genuine illness, just like the flu?

Did you know that *depression* comes in many forms, whether it be clinical *depression*, bipolar, postpartum or even a relatively new one recently identified – *smile depression*. Yes, you read correctly, *smile depression* and while I have firsthand experienced some of the others mentioned above as well, I can honestly tell you, *smile depression* is now a big concern of mine!

ARE YOU HIDING BEHIND A 'FORCED' SMILE?

Think about it. Usually, when you think of someone suffering from *depression*, they are friends who are noticeably sad and perhaps disengaged from their loved ones and everyday life. Possibly you can relate to this.

You, on the other hand, *smile* all day long — at work, playing with your kids and/or grandkids, with your spouse and when greeting others at the cashier's line in the grocery store. *You laugh, you smile, and you may 'look' happy.* Yet you can't seem to shake off the feelings of loneliness and sadness that are buried deep below your surface

DO YOU HAVE SMILE DEPRESSION?

According to **Thai-An Truong**, a mental health therapist at Oklahoma's **Lasting Change Therapy**, this is *smiling depression,* also known as perfectly hidden depression. Symptoms include similar to those of depression: low mood, sadness, low self-worth, isolation and hopelessness. Is this you?

Do you **"put on a happy face in front of others"**, hiding your vulnerability and even using laughter as a means to disguise your pain? Don't deny it any longer if you suffer or know someone who does.

It's this very reason that people, especially women, with *smiling depression* who look put-together on the outside avoid getting help. You may feel like '*oh this too will pass*' and isn't bad enough to warrant reaching out to get help or see a mental health professional.

REACHING OUT FOR HELP

The good news is that help is actually closer than you think. The first step is to get yourself out of denial. Acknowledge that what you're feeling is *"real".* Next, talk to someone you trust. It can be a family member, someone you work with, a fellow church member or your primary care physician. Let them know what's going on.

And listen carefully… If they discount your feelings, find SOMEONE ELSE. You must be your own self-advocate!

Sure eating a better diet and getting daily exercise can obviously help too. But you know what. So does *therapy*.

And please, if you know of a friend or a family member who seems to have it all turns to you for comfort, please don't dismiss them. Don't tell them to be grateful for what they have.

Instead, let that person know that you're there to listen and *suppor* them. This goes for everyone suffering any type of *depression*.

USE SOCIAL MEDIA TO REACH OUT TOO!

With the modern technology of today, there's not a better time than to take advantage of using social media! You know and I know, we all like to hear that familiar *ding'* announcing to us to let us know someone is sending a message. Call, text, Facebook, zoom, or even email your friend(s) and engage with them in a meaningful conversation! And yes, don't forget to address them by their name. This is important, people feel *'special'* when you call them by their name.

For some people, messaging via social media allows you to 'open up' more than you would have if in person. Not everyone, but for those who are somewhat introverted, this is an excellent option to help you who may need this type of engagement to connect and have meaningful dialogue.

And remember, you know you're getting thru once you see that all too familiar smiley face icon!?!

WHAT CAN MAKE ME HAPPY AGAIN?

You can learn how to shake off your feelings of sadness and start feeling happy again. You no longer have to feel this way. You DESERVE to be happy and below we're going to discuss 5 effective ways to bring happiness back into your life!

5 WAYS TO GET BACK TO HAPPY!

By learning these five simple steps, you will help get your *smile* to resurface by putting YOU first. You will see how easy it is to love yourself back to being able to *smile again*.

Once you have mastered these *five simple steps*, the benefits will help you achieve better overall well-being and greater happiness. So, grab a pencil (okay, maybe your iPad…), take notes and let's begin, shall we?

1.   ***You must live in the present***. Stop replaying negative events over and over again in your head. And don't worry about the future. It hasn't even arrived yet… Learn to be grateful for everything good in your life. Accept and celebrate the flexibility of nature. Be open to the serendipity nature of the ebbs and flow of everything around you and appreciate the *"small stuff"*. And finally, take a step back and observe yourself in the moment. Instead of always 'reacting' to whatever you're confronting, 'respond' and learn how to approach life in more harmoniously.

2.   ***Let go of negative thoughts.*** You *must* learn to forgive and forget and simply move on. Holding a grudge takes so much emotional and physical energy. It's not worth it. Forgiveness allows YOU to exchange that negative energy into something more positive for yourself. It's ***'freeing'***. Embrace failures

or, mistakes and allow yourself to open up to success. Realize just how unique and special you truly are. Try to spend less time pleasing others and more time pleasing your higher self. Remove 'toxic' people from your life and hang out with *like-minded, positive-oriented friends* and family members.

3. *Be kind.* Another way of finding happiness to get your smile back is to simply follow the golden rule: *"Do unto others as you would have them do to you".* How about doing a random act of kindness. Go out of your way to help someone. You have no idea how much happiness and self-worth you can gain. It can be as easy as giving a bottle of water to a homeless person or paying a simple compliment to anyone you come in contact with. Even if it's a total stranger. Kindness is also about being respectful to others. Sometimes it's just better to let the other person be right once in a while. And when you do this simple action, you will *SMILE back* inside of yourself and immediately feel humbled and blessed for doing so.

4. *Get healthy and get an active lifestyle.* I know you've heard it said many times, but it is true. Exercise really does make you feel better. It releases those wonderful endorphins which in turn helps you to relieve stress, minimize depression and improve your mood. You can't help but be happier after a great workout that makes you sweat. Make a conscious effort to eat healthily. You know what I'm talking about. Keep it clean and be sure to drink as much water as necessary to stay hydrated. And finally, take some time 'off' from being on your cell phone and checking Facebook or whatever every other minute! Don't be distracted all of the time. Stay focused, pray, meditate, do yoga, anything that helps you reflect and makes you feel better for your sense of well-being.

5.   **_Laugh more and you will smile more._** You've heard it before but I'm going to remind you anyway. Laughter *IS* the best medicine. It too releases those feel-good endorphins. When was the last time you had a really good laugh? I'm talking a deep down 'belly laugh'! If you haven't seen the YouTube version of the delightful **'Chewbacca Lady'**, here's your chance now to not only see it but really get into it and have yourself a 'belly laugh' as well. You'll be grinning from ear to ear with the biggest smile ever. You'll thank me later, trust me!

RECLAIM YOUR JOY AND HAPPINESS!

Don't let your sadness rob you of the true joys of life. You deserve to have your 'inside' match what you show on the outside. And one of the goals of creating *'Made You Smile Back'* is to have a place to go to talk about things of this matter and to leave with a 'smile', a genuine 'smile back'.

I've survived this before...
I'm stronger than I realize... This feeling will pass.
- Beth Elkassih, Author

CHAPTER TWO

GIGGLE, LAUGH & BE SILLY ONCE IN A WHILE!

Giggle, laugh and be silly once in a while! I am so excited to present this fun and delightful article about keeping your sense of humor.

It's okay to giggle, laugh and be silly once in a while.
- Beth Elkassih, Author

In this chapter, we will explore why laughter is indeed the best medicine and will reveal seven signs that demonstrate a good sense of humor. You shall learn all the incredible health benefits one receives and of course the 'best of the best' jokes and tidbits will be shared as well!

So! Who's ready to read a new chapter where you are guaranteed to be smiling back when you're finished!

WHAT DOES A SENSE OF HUMOR MEAN?

What does a sense of humor mean anyway? It's someone who often finds things amusing or funny rather than being serious all the time. I believe we all are born with a sense of humor. Don't believe me? Go to YouTube and type in 'laughing babies'!

A sense of humor is built into every human's brain. It sets us apart from at least most other animals. It is a skill of survival and shows up even in dire situations. Of course, depending upon our personality, one's sense of humor defines the real you…. and cannot be faked.

HISTORICALLY SPEAKING...

Think for a moment. Can you even imagine living without a sense of humor? A world void of laughter or the ability to smile? You can't because it's simply not possible. It's part of our DNA and human evolution.

Who isn't familiar with court jesters? Throughout history, jesters played a significant role in ancient history and were entertainers usually dressed in colorful garments. Early jesters were popular in Ancient Egypt and entertained Egyptian pharaohs.

Jesters were also popular with the Aztec people in the 14th to 16th centuries as with the Roman Empire. Perhaps they are best known in British England where many royal courts throughout English royal history employed entertainers and most had professional fools, sometimes called licensed fools whose simple job was to make people laugh.

Here's the deal… if someone can say or do something to evoke another person to smile or laugh… it proves without a doubt that 'everyone' has a sense of humor. Its strong attraction is like a magnet and unites people for the common good.

LAUGHTER IS THE BEST MEDICINE

We all need to 'lighten up' a bit, don't you think? Let's take a moment and recall joyful faces of laughter from 'happy-go-lucky' children when innocently Remind yourself of how it felt being unconditionally happy and joyful as a child.

The benefits of laughter, being silly, giggling, and just plain being funny is indisputable. Learn the simple power of laughter and humor. It's fun to share a good laugh and it's true, laughter is strong medicine.

It draws people together and strengthens your immune system. It helps our mental health when dealing with and coping with problems of everyday life. Laughter has the power to transform fear of the unknown into enthusiasm for new possibilities. Take a look at all the following health benefits we derive from being 'silly'!

THE BENEFITS OF LAUGHTER & HUMOR

Physical Health Benefits

- Boosts immunity
- Lowers stress hormones
- Decreases pain
- Relaxes your muscles
- Prevents heart disease

Mental Health Benefits

- Adds joy and zest to life
- Eases anxiety and tension
- Relieves stress
- Improves mood
- Strengthens resilience

Social Benefits

- Strengthens relationships
- Attracts others to us
- Enhances teamwork
- Helps defuse conflict
- Promotes group bonding

TYPES OF SENSE OF HUMOR

Before we dive into what the seven signs are of having a good sense of humor, we first need to discuss the obvious… there are different 'types' of sense of humor. Humor greatly differs from one person to another. Who doesn't have a cousin, or an uncle, or friend that always seems to have a dark sense of humor or one who is sharp-witted or even those who are just plain 'silly' all the time!

Psychologist Rod Martin, went out to determine and quantify humor and in 2003 he identified what he called the four broad styles of humor:

1. Affiliative
2. Self-enhancing
3. Aggressive
4. Self-defeating

According to the **Journal of Research in Personality,** Martin describes these 4 styles of humor: "Affiliative humor, he said, is used "to enhance one's relationships with others," and involves engaging in banter and cracking jokes with friends. Self-enhancing humor involves making yourself feel better by finding humor in your situation. Aggressive humor is marked by sarcasm, teasing, and ridicule, and self-defeating humor involves putting yourself down to gain approval from others.

Going further, Martin explains that virtually everyone's sense of humor is a blend of different humor styles, but many people tend to lean in one direction. Nevertheless, there is a definite difference in between a 'good and healthy sense of humor' versus someone who is simply 'mean-spirited'.

If you could choose one characteristic that would get you through life, choose a sense of humor..
- Beth Elkassih, Author

SIGNS YOU HAVE A GOOD & HEALTHY SENSE OF HUMOR

Do **YOU** have an amazing sense of humor? Are you the type of person that can walk into a room full of people and just make everyone laugh and smile with no effort at all?

If so, you are to be envied, because these are the type of people we all like to hang out with. Why not? Because it makes you feel happy, right? The 7 signs of a good and healthy sense of humor are:

1. **You make laughing a priority.** Those who have a good sense of humor not only see the value in making others laugh, but they prioritize laughter themselves. And as a result, they're healthier and happier for it.

2. **You practice self-acceptance.** Not everyone can be like **Ellen Degeneres,** but those of us who have a light-hearted attitude do practice more self-acceptance than most. Good-humored individuals embrace their flaws and laugh them off (and let them go) in a healthy way. Self-acceptance is *key to a happier life.*

3. **More than likely you are a creative individual.** These individuals can think on their feet and are known for their humorous quick wit. Having a creative mind also lends itself to having sharper short-term memory with their healthy dose of laughter daily.

4. **You're more conscientious and have compassion and empathy.** There's a fine line between mean-spirited jokes and well-intentioned humor, and those with good humor know the difference. You can be

funny and be kind, and make people laugh without the expense of hurting somebody.

5. **More than likely, you are in great physical shape and possess positive well-being.** When you exercise and are fit, the endorphins act as a stimulant that lends itself to confidence and that all-important well-being. According to Peter McGraw, Ph.D., an associate professor at the University of Colorado Boulder who studies emotions. "[W]hen done well, humor can have a significant positive effect on your life," .he wrote for **Psychology Today.**

6. **It's the secret sauce in having great relationships.** A well-timed funny meme can do a lot of good. It has often been said, "Laughter is good for the soul." Why not apply that to both business and social relationships?

7. **Aging is just a 'fact of life' to you.** Good-humored individuals don't let birthdays get them down. They take it all in stride. Their light-hearted nature may help you live longer. Research suggests that a *sense of humor increases longevity into retirement.* So bring it, birthdays!!!

Laughter is the best form of medicine!
- Beth Elkassih

99

ARE YOU READY TO LAUGH? 10 JOKES THAT WILL MAKE YOU SMILE BACK!

1. "I used to think I was indecisive, but now I'm not too sure...!!!"

2. "I am often asked, is **GOOGLE** a man or a woman? My simple answer is 'it's a woman because it won't let you finish your sentence without making a suggestion...!!!...'"

3. "Before Instagram, I used to waste so much time sitting around having to imagine what my friends' food looked like...!!!..."

4. "My wife isn't talking to me because apparently I ruined her birthday... I'm not sure how I did that — I didn't even know it was her birthday...!!!..."

5. "A client calls the hotline of an internet service provider: 'I have a problem, my internet stopped working two days ago, neither I nor my son nor anyone else can access it now...' 'I see, do you know what's the operating system on your PC?'..... 'Of course I do! It's Facebook...!!!...'"

6. "My boss told me to have a good day... so I went home...!!!...."

7. "Did you hear about the Italian chef that died? He pasta way..!!!..

8. "Knock, knock. Who's there? Britney Spears. Britney Spears who? Knock, knock – Oops I did it again...!!!..."

9. "Don't use "beef stew" as a computer password. It's not stroganoff...!!!..."

10. "Knock, knock. Who's there? MadeYa. MadeYa who? Made You Smile Back...!!!...

Wait! There's More!

GIGGLE, LAUGH & BE SILLY ONCE IN AWHILE!

How many of you remember the viral Facebook video of the 'Chewbacca Lady'? Well, believe it or not, her name is Candace Payne and she lives just 25 minutes from me in Grand Prairie, TX. I just couldn't end this chapter without recommending you go visit her online YouTube video. Just Google search 'Chewbacca Lady'. For those of you who remember, you will laugh again... For those of you who have no idea what I'm talking about... then you're in for a real treat! I GUARANTEE you will laugh so hard, you will have tears in your eyes!?!

Humor is gifts of blessings.

- Beth Elkassih

CHAPTER THREE

FEELING LONELY? 7 SECRET TECHNIQUES FOR DEALING WITH LONELINESS

'Finding Your Way 'Out of the Dark'

Do you often find yourself feeling lonely? I don't know about you, but there have been more than a few times in my life where I just felt so alone. And what makes matters worse, oftentimes I have felt that I had no one to go to when I felt those bouts of loneliness. Don't you wish there were some secret tips you could apply for dealing with or better yet, eliminate loneliness?

Seven effective secret techniques will be shared for dealing with loneliness and get back to feeling happy. Every human being goes through periods of feeling lonely. But if these feelings continue unchecked, then you can easily find yourself suffering from a mental health disease that is very real. And can even shorten your life!

We shall discuss exactly what loneliness is and how it is caused, explain the difference between being alone vs loneliness, the most common types of loneliness and present strategies in coping and finding your way 'out of the darkness'.

FACT: LONELINESS IS A WORLDWIDE EPIDEMIC CURRENTLY AFFECTING 1 IN EVERY 3 ADULTS

Loneliness impacts your physical health just as much as being overweight or smoking cigarettes.

- Beth Elkassih

WHAT EXACTLY IS LONELINESS?

According to verywellmind.com, loneliness is described as a state of solitude or being alone. But actually, loneliness is a state of mind. Loneliness causes people to feel empty, alone, and unwanted. Lonely people often crave human contact, but their state of mind makes it more difficult to form connections with other people.

On the other hand, loneliness is not necessarily about being alone. Instead, if you feel alone and isolated, then that is how loneliness plays into your state of mind. But wait, some people are known to be 'loners'. How does this play out?

Sometimes the person who tries to keep everyone happy is the most lonely person.

- Unknown

THE DIFFERENCE BETWEEN BEING A 'LONER' VS BEING 'LONELY'

Everyone's experience with loneliness is different from one another. It's a personal thing. We must recognize that loneliness is not often the same thing and quite differently from being alone.

In fact, many people freely choose to be alone and live quite content and happy. Others may find this to be rather lonely. But even 'loners' can easily find themselves struggling with loneliness as well.

There is a distinct difference between feeling lonely versus feeling alone. It's amazing how you can feel "lonely" in a crowd of people and likewise, quite content and peaceful when alone at home.

- Beth Elkassih

ARE YOU A LONELY SOCIALITE?

Are you a Social Loner? How many of you would be labeled easily by your friends who 'think they know you' and would argue that you're one of the most social people out there! Often you're considered the life of the party, right? Sound familiar? Let's go one step further, shall we?

We can be totally surrounded by people — regardless of whether they are family, friends or strangers and we still feel so very much alone. Is it any wonder that even well-known celebrities and personalities have suffered all their life dealing with this condition?

Yes, it is with much sadness that the world lost the most comedic and heart-warming soul — Robin Williams. He recently passed three years ago, on August 11, 2015. He suffered from major depression which was the result of isolation and loneliness, especially in his later years. The problem with being a 'social loner' is the fact that it's even more difficult, in the eyes of these special people, to reach out and seek help…. much-needed help.

In the following paragraphs, I shall go into more detail on the symptoms, causes and effects of loneliness. It is SO IMPORTANT that you fully understand the depth and scope of this real, if not potentially dangerous disease.

SYMPTOMS OF LONELINESS

Are you feeling disconnected? As mentioned earlier, symptoms of loneliness may differ from person to person but may take on one or more of the symptoms as featured on Psych2Go. Psych2Go is a popular YouTube channel that currently has over 2.4 million subscribers and promotes mental health advocacy. They list these 7 symptoms of loneliness:

1. Your insomnia is an ongoing problem. According to research published in the journal Sleep, loneliness can wreck your chances of getting a restful night's sleep. Researchers measured the sleep cycles of 95 people in South

Dakota, comparing them with the participant's self-reported loneliness scores. The results? The lonelier the participant, the higher the levels of fragmented sleep.

2. **Your anxiety worsens.** Do you already suffer from anxiety? When you are lonely, anxiety increases your cortisol based on your stress levels In turn, you will also start to have more feelings of hopelessness and become even more isolated by feeling 'locked in' to our home or one favorite spot. You may also find yourself lounging all day in your pj's or even begin binge-watching your favorite NetFlix shows.

3. **You have difficulty with social situations**. Research shows that people who are lonely have a harder time understanding and adapting social skills. Thus, they become isolated and even more alone.

4. **You choose materials over people**. According to research published in the Journal of Consumer Research, some people go gaga over inanimate objects because they're lonely. The researchers call this "material possession love," and you've probably witnessed many times: your neighbor who calls his car "baby," or your great aunt who prides herself on her doll collection. Because these folks suffer from a lack of social connections, they start doting on their things. Obviously, material items cannot buy you happiness versus having real-life experiences interacting and connecting with friends and family.

5. **You're gaining weight.** When you're lonely, you find yourself turning to 'comfort food' or eating out of boredom. If you don't catch yourself early on to break the cycle, the calories add up…

6. **Alone time doesn't feel fun anymore!** If you start to feel more irritable than usual or you have no one to talk to who can relate to you like in the past, you may realize that alone time is no longer enjoyable as it once was, especially if you consider yourself a loner by choice.

Once you recognize that you may have one or more of these symptoms, you need to reach out to your primary care physician and determine what is causing you this distress.

WHAT CAUSES LONELINESS ANYWAY?!?

Loneliness is a real and overwhelming problem that people struggle with every day. We know what the symptoms are, but what causes loneliness in the first place? Let's find out.

1. A new move or relocation to a new city or country. As a result, you suddenly have no friends to turn to when needed.

2. Becoming a newlywed or Mom and suddenly your old 'single friends' seem to have abandoned you.

3. You've become newly divorced or separated and find yourself having to make new friends becoming even more isolated.

4. Unlike becoming a new mother, a stay-at-home mom can feel that her career-driven friends have vanished from her inner circle.

5. People who suffer from anxiety, self-esteem issues or weight-related issues all can contribute to loneliness as well.

6. If you're suffering from current mental health issues or battling chronic illnesses, these conditions can trigger loneliness and isolation from others who 'simply don't understand' what you're going through.

7. Perhaps your very best friend moved a long distance away or you recently endured a relationship break-up. You find yourself having too much time on your hands and thus loneliness creeps in.

8. Empathetically and understandingly, we would be amiss if we didn't include the sorrowful bereavement of losing a loved one. In fact, research from Dr. R.S. Weiss, PhD., there is a strong preponderance of evidence to support that one can actually 'die' of a broken heart and loneliness as a result of the death of your spouse. It's important to have close family friends be nearby so you can reach out to them as needed and as for as long as you need to!

THE SHOCKING EFFECTS OF LONELINESS AND HOW OUR BODY REACTS

Loneliness and isolation can have far-reaching effects on our health, whether they occur together or independently of each other. Let's take a closer look at both the physical and mental effects that loneliness causes.

The vicious cycle of loneliness -- 'My mental health has made me lonely'...==> 'Feeling lonely has damaged my mental health'.

- Beth Elkassih, Author

HEALTH RISKS ASSOCIATED WITH LONELINESS

A 2017 review Trusted Source of 40 studies on social isolation and loneliness found evidence to link these states to a higher risk of early death, cardiovascular issues, and worsened mental health.

Another 2017 Study Trusted Source looked at results from the **2012 Swiss Health Survey,** and found evidence to link loneliness to increased risk for:

- chronic illness
- high cholesterol
- emotional distress
- diabetes
- depression

7 SECRET TECHNIQUES TO COPE WITH LONELINESS

So enough already! Do you not agree on how important it is that we learn to take care of ourselves and treat loneliness as a real health concern? We need to treat it as it truly is -- a bonafide medical disease. I encourage each and everyone reading this to learn these seven secret tips to cope with and help eliminate loneliness

1. Acceptance that you are lonely. Dissect your feelings about it – change the mindset from having no friends to making friends.

2. Make a plan to deal with the loneliness – go where people are – like a coffee shop or the mall or the library – chat in lines – engage in small talk.

3. Get outside – an immediate mood booster – take a daily walk in a scenic park. Nature is so healing and you will feel an instant connection.

4. Start an exercise program – a dance class – the combo of music and movement will release the feel-good hormones – leaving you feeling more positive and energetic. Plus this is a great way to meet new friends!

5. Journal, journal, journal. I can't emphasize the importance of pouring it all out there in a journal. Start doing daily and over time, you will progress from 'venting' to determining meaningful and effective solutions.

6. Create a support network of people to call or text or do facetime when feeling down.

7. Seek out counseling, therapy and/or make an immediate appointment with your primary care provider.

BOTTOM LINE

The big 'takeaway' from this article is… Remember, loneliness is temporary. Even if you're feeling lonely now, that doesn't mean you'll always feel lonely or you'll never find a community that nourishes you.

You are the architect of your future. You get to go out and make new and wise choices.

Every one of us has something to offer in all the connections and relationships we make. You've just got to go out and create them!

- Beth Elkassih, Author

CHAPTER FOUR

SIX TRAITS ALL HAPPY & SUCCESSFUL PEOPLE HAVE PLUS... THE MOST SECRET 7TH TRAIT REVEALED!

Discover how you can develop seven traits that all happy and successful people have PLUS reveal the most secret of them all!

So what are we waiting for! Let's begin our discovery. Would it surprise you at all to know that the same brilliant Nobel Peace Prize winner, **Albert Einstein** is known for his Theory of Relativity is also credited for creating a Theory for Happiness!

The Theory for Happiness was comprised of just two simple paragraphs that Einstein wrote while in Japan waiting for a lecture. In fact, those 2 autographed notes on Einstein's thoughts on how to live a happy and fulfilled life, sold at a Jerusalem auction house a couple of years ago for a combined $1.8 million dollars!

'A calm and modest life brings more happiness than the pursuit of success combined with constant restlessness.' and 'Where there's a will, there's a way.'

-Albert Einstein

Let's also take a moment and reflect on what **Norman Vincent Peale** had to say about happiness and success.

> *Believe in yourself! Have faith in your abilities!*
> *Without a humble but reasonable confidence in your*
> *own powers, you cannot be successful or happy.*
> *-Norman Vincent Peale*

HAPPY & SUCCESSFUL PEOPLE LEAVE BEHIND 'CLUES'!

Want to know *why* happy people are successful? Fortunately, happy and successful people leave plenty of clues on why they are who they are. There are definitely certain traits or characteristics one observes easily from them.

Let's examine the qualities of happiness versus successful habits they possess:

- Happy people easily let things go and forgive and forget. Successful people see problems merely as opportunities in disguise.

- Happy people have huge dreams. Successful people simply dream big always.

- Happy people are kind and treat people as they would treat others (i.e. Golden Rule). Successful people respect their fellow colleagues and are open to new ideas for their personal development and growth.

- Happy people easily express gratitude. Successful people always acknowledge their peers and seek out 'mentors' to whom they are grateful.

WANT TO KNOW 'WHY' HAPPY PEOPLE ARE SUCCESSFUL?

- Happy people always find the 'good' in others. Successful people always know his/her own strengths.
- Happy people take full responsibility for their life and what happens. Successful people embrace full responsibility and see failures or mishaps as learning experiences that move them forward towards ultimate success.
- Happy people live in the present moment. Successful people are always planning ahead with Plan B or C. They live in the moment, yes, but they always have their eye on their future.
- Happy people surround themselves with other happy people. Successful people surround themselves with other successful people.
- Happy people have high self-esteem and confidence. Successful people also exhibit strong self-esteem and confidence and in addition, constantly seek out knowledge.

HAPPINESS + SUCCESS = Love of Life and

Outstanding Achievement.

-Beth Elkassih, Author

99

MORE QUALITIES THAT HAPPY & SUCCESSFUL PEOPLE SHARE

There are so many qualities we just can't overlook. Here are some more:

- Happy people do not seek nor need the approval of others. Likewise, successful people also don't take 'no' for an answer.

- Happy people are honest. Successful people have integrity.

- Both happy and successful people are good listeners. They listen to 'understand' not with the intent to 'reply'.

- Happy people change what they can and accept what they cannot. Successful people easily prioritize their goals and don't sweat the small stuff.

- Together, both happy & successful people choose their destiny.

- Both happy and successful people also have strong faith in their own individual spirituality and/or religion. This can not be overlooked.

Is it any wonder that the happiest people are also the most successful people?

SIX POWERFUL TRAITS PEOPLE WHO ARE BOTH HAPPY & SUCCESSFUL MUST HAVE

I know traits are also known as personality characteristics and even the qualities mentioned above go a long way in determining who we are as a person. But what are the more important traits in others who are both happy and successful? Let's dive in deeper and explore.

1. They are both 'intrinsically driven'. According to Andreo Corso, Contributing Editor for **Huffington Post**, "their inspiration and drive come from within. It's not about money, title, or anything external or material. It's about how what they're doing feels to them. Does it make them happy? It is serving a purpose? Are they serving others? If the answers are yes, they keep going. And if not, they don't. They know their joy and enthusiasm for what they're doing and how they're living life is contagious and inspires others. That motivates them to continue to live joyfully and enthusiastically. " Their self-discipline is evident and nothing is possible without it.

2. They both 'believe in their dreams'. To be both happy and successful, the key is to believe in yourself when no one else does. If you listen to your critics you can't achieve what you want. Be relentless in the pursuit of your goals and never listen to your critics.

3. They both have 'resilience'. Angela Lee Duckworth of the **University of Pennsylvania** says that grit is the single quality that guarantees success,

based on her ground-breaking studies. Talent will not take the place of persistence and resilience. As Ms. Duckworth further explained, "Steve Jobs is a great example of this. He was fired from the company he started but in his wilderness, he started another company NeXT and bought Pixar. Then he patiently waited for his second coming to Apple and as they say, the rest is history. You can be down but never out "

4. They both have 'passion' Passion ignites reservoirs of resilience. It is the fuel in which a happy and successful person uses toward skyrocketing towards their goals. They are not afraid of hard work and know that 'practice' makes perfect. They look at 'failures' as part of the process and take every opportunity to learn and move forward. And as Richard Marcinko says, "The more you sweat in training, the less you bleed in combat."

5. They both take care of themselves better, both physically and mentally. The simple truth is happy and successful people take care of themselves better. They try to ensure that they have proper rest and balance in their lives. If you want to achieve all you want out of your life you need to ensure that you are at your best most of the time. Energy is required to go forward towards your closely cherished dreams. Besides, these wonderful people also maintain a positive mental attitude. Being grateful for what we have while striving for more is actually a great way to stay positive. When you are positive about the day you just get on with the accomplishment of your tasks with even more vigor. Furthermore, nothing is more important than your inner peace and overall happiness.

6. They both have exceptional 'communication skills'. Clarity is the key to communicating effectively. The happy and successful person knows how to listen to 'what is not heard', listens to 'understand' and can easily 'empathize' with others.

THE SECRET 7TH TRAIT OF HAPPY & SUCCESSFUL PEOPLE IS...

Mernell King Director of Training for GreenLight Training LLC, says it ell:

"If you don't ask, you won't get..."

This is the secret and in my mind, the most highly desirable trait that a appy and successful person can have. Yes, they tend to be 'risk-takers' but in trategic ways.

Think about it. I witnessed this trait first-hand for the past year from omeone who I regard as both happy and successful. I discovered 'why' this trait both powerful and effective. Again, successful people are NOT AFRAID to SK! So... why is this so valuable?

Here's the deal folks... If you ask for something and put 'yourself out ere', you will NEVER KNOW what opportunities are awaiting you. If you ask, en who knows, the answer may be a resounding 'sure, why not!' Or... if you ask, erhaps the response may be, 'I can't do that for you, but I CAN DO THIS FOR

YOU!' And you know what, perhaps THIS response will provide even more potential opportunities better than the simple yes!

Of course, you can also get a 'no' for an answer.... but how will you know UNLESS YOU ASK! This, my friends, is the secret trait that you must all learn to develop and have. Put yourself out there. You have nothing to lose but 'everything' to gain.

IN SUMMARY, THE 7 TOTAL TRAITS OF HAPPY & SUCCESSFUL PEOPLE

So, how would YOU like to learn how you too can become not only a happier person but a successful one as well? To recap, strive to do all these 7 'must-have' traits:

1. **Be Intrinsically Driven.**

2. **Believe in Your Dreams.**

3. **Be Resilient.**

4. **Be Passionate and Hard-Working.**

5. **Practice Self-Care and Maintain a Positive Attitude.**

6. **Develop Exceptional Communication Skills — Effective Listening and Empathy.**

I would like to take this opportunity to do a 'shout out' to Umair Qureshi creator of **WPSTAIRS** and Founder/Owner of **Zulzan.** He is my web-developer graphics designer and consultant for my professional blog, **Made You Smile**

Back. It is through working and observing this brilliant gentleman in the past year that I discovered and learned about this 'secret 7th trait' of what it takes to be both truly happy and successful.

HAPPINESS + SUCCESS = Love of Life and Outstanding Achievement.
-Beth Elkassih, Author

CHAPTER FIVE

HOW HAPPY ARE YOU REALLY?

Everyday people just want to be happy. Have you ever wondered just how happy you really are? I'm so excited to introduce a unique and thought-provoking blog to dive in and explore this emotion we know as 'happiness'. Let's find out what really makes you smile back!

In my assessment, happiness is much more than just an attitude. It's a combination of positivity, spirituality and a healthy dose of optimism. Sure, we all have our ups and downs. That is just the way life is. But your level of happiness will directly correlate to your overall well-being and mental health.

When you have the right 'Happiness Quotient', you can more easily navigate the demands of everyday life. In this article, I will first describe two of the more popular 'psychological happiness tests or questionnaires' that are currently used today in a clinical setting. Then I will provide you with an inside look at **Martin Seligman's** popular self-help book, **'Authentic Happiness'.**

The second part of this unique two-part blog concerns finding out individually what our 'authentic level of happiness' is. There shall be an enlightening, but fun quiz you may sign up for to get a more personal view of your own happiness level or what MYSB (aka **Made You Smile Back**) refers to as the 'Happiness Quotient'.

To access this quiz, simply search for this URL link in your preferred web browser: **https://madeyousmileback.com/happiness-quiz**

So let's get our happiness levels going in the right direction, shall we?...

DEFINITION OF HAPPINESS

What better place to start our discussion about what happiness really is than by surfing straight to the ultimate internet resource, **Wikipedia**:

Happiness is used in the context of mental or emotional states, including positive or pleasant emotions ranging from contentment to intense joy. It is also used in the context of life satisfaction, subjective well-being, flourishing and well-being.

Wikipedia

Wikipedia goes on to say that 'Happiness' is often the subject of debate of usage and/or meaning and even subtle differences in understanding in various cultures.

For instance when observing happy children blowing soap bubbles or playing in the water, in the context of current experience, one can experience the feeling of high emotion, also known as pleasure or joy. You can see it also as a more general sense of 'emotional condition' as a whole.

Others may view 'happiness' as a type of an appraisal measurement of 'quality of life'. For instance, Ruut Veenhoven has defined happiness as "overall appreciation of one's life as-a-whole."

In the academic world, happiness is often described as subjective well-being, which includes measures of affect and life satisfaction. For instance, **Sonja Lyubomirsky** has described happiness as "the experience of joy, contentment, or positive well-being, combined with a sense that one's life is good, meaningful, and worthwhile."

Finally, happiness is often translated into flourishing and having an overall feeling of well-being.

These uses can give different results. For instance, the correlation of income levels has been shown to be substantial with life satisfaction measures. Whereas someone involved in an unconditionally loving relationship can be viewed as a pure emotional condition of well-being.

DO YOU KNOW THE 4 LEVELS OF HAPPINESS?

Per the **Spitzer Center for Visionary Leadership®**, the 'Four Levels of Happiness' are based upon the essence of timeless principles going clear back to **Aristotle**. **Aristotle** is well known for his philosophical viewpoint that 'happiness is the one thing we desire in and of itself, everything else is desired for the sake of happiness". Let's take a closer look at these four levels of happiness.

SPITZER'S® FOUR LEVELS OF HAPPINESS

1. The first level of happiness is basically what is known as immediate gratification. We derive pleasure out of simple impulsive desires. The

problem is that it is short-lived, shallow and impacts no one else except ourselves.

2. The second level of happiness is more evident in the satisfaction of our egos. We all strive to be recognized in our career, constantly achieving and winning to get ahead. This level of happiness is also short-term because one can easily get 'stuck' at this level and never be satisfied with what they have accomplished. This level is not enduring.

3. The third level of happiness is still about winning, and somewhat ego-driven as well. But the difference is that level three is aimed at 'serving others'. It's about wanting to make a contribution or a difference in the world around us. This is long-term in nature and very gratifying.

4. The final and fourth level of happiness is what we all want to finally achieve. The ultimate goal is not found in materialistic things. But rather in the fundamental yearning for perfect truth, beauty, love, goodness, and being. This level of happiness correlates to our own personal spiritual beliefs and is the 'Ultimate Good' and is both self-sustaining and enduring.

If you are too busy to laugh... you are too busy.

-Proverb

AUTHENTIC HAPPINESS

Martin E. P. Seligman is a well known and influential Psychologist who is well known for writing several self-help books. His most popular one is 'Authentic Happiness' written in 2002.

This book has been a classic in positive psychology. The book is divided into 3 parts: **'Positive Emotion, Strength and Virtue'**. **Seligman** also identifies six core virtues or positive traits that can increase well-being. They are:

SIX CORE VIRTUES

- Wisdom
- Courage
- Love/Humanity
- Justice
- Temperance
- Spirituality/Transcendence

Authentic happiness comes from identifying and cultivating your most fundamental strengths and using them every day in work, love, play and parenting.

-Martin E.P. Seligman

The third part of the book deals with the question, "What is the good life?" In terms of work and life satisfaction, happiness has little to do with money. Across studies, freedom of choice and experiences of flow are much more impacting.

So… are you ready to take the next step in becoming a better and happier person? Let's find out how happy you really are! If you're ready, enter this URL link in your web browser:

https://madeyousmileback.com/happiness-quiz

CHAPTER SIX

THE TRUE VALUE OF FRIENDSHIP & HAPPINESS
The Value of Friendship

When is the last time you had a genuine conversation with a close friend? Regardless of the content of your discussion, you felt better afterward, right? And more importantly, it did indeed contribute to your overall level of happiness as well.

I am so pleased to discuss this ever-important quality of the value of friendship and how it affects our happiness. You will discover what friendship is really about, types of friendship, benefits of friendship, and how happiness plays an important role in our relationships.

True friendship promotes the good and happiness

of one another.

-Eustace Budgell

WHAT EXACTLY DOES FRIENDSHIP MEAN?

Friendship is the innate need for all mankind to feel a belonging or a connection to one another. According to **Kendra Cherry, MS**, it refers to a human emotional need to affiliate with and be accepted. But it's a lot more than just that.

What everyone needs to know about the value of friendship is its strong correlation to our state of happiness and well-being. It's a known fact after many studies, that friendship not only boosts our health but our happiness as well.

True friends are those who are there for you not just for the good times, but when times are not so good. True friends are reciprocal to one another and bring out the best of the best in each other. True friends demonstrate the real definition of being nonjudgmental and what unconditional love really means.

FOUR TRAITS OF TRUE FRIENDSHIP

- **Reliability** — Being reliable builds trust – your friends and loved ones know that they can count on you to keep your word, be there when you'll say you'll be, and do what you say you'll do. Reliability also shows respect for each other.

- **Listening & Being Nonjudgmental** — Non–judgmental listening means listening to understand and put your views and values aside and being careful not to criticize or judge the person who you are listening to. It means accepting them as a person and accepting the things that they are struggling with.

- **Authenticity** — Authenticity is about the presence and staying true to yourself. Showing your 'colors' no matter what when you're with your friends. An authentic person puts their friends around them at ease, in a comforting way and makes one feels as if they are at home.

- **Trustworthy** — The definition of trustworthy is someone honest who can be entrusted with your secrets and knowing they won't be shared with anyone else. It's also considered to be one of the most important traits of true friendship. You don't need someone who is going to agree with you all the time. You need that special friend who you trust to be upfront and tell you what they really are thinking. To hear the advice they are sharing with you.

FRIENDSHIPS THROUGHOUT LIFE

Childhood friends were the best, right? Childhood friendship is innocent, free from care and it is unconditional. If you're lucky enough, you may even have developed a lifelong friend sealed with a pinkie promise!

Friendships are incredibly important during the formidable teen years, otherwise known as adolescence. Teen friendships help young people feel a sense of acceptance and belonging.

Moreover, teenage relationships with peers support the development of compassion, caring, and empathy. Furthermore, adolescent friendships are a big part of forming a sense of identity outside the family.

That said, teen friendships can also, unfortunately, have a dark side and team up with friends who are simply 'fake'. It's important to be able to recognize the traits of toxic friends. Usually, one knows immediately simply for the mere fact that spending time with them doesn't make you feel good. And remember, true friendship is one that promotes your happiness and well-being.

CAUTION – BE AWARE OF **TOXIC FRIENDSHIPS** – THEY ARE NOT YOUR FRIENDS – LEARN TO WALK AWAY.

Moving into our college years, and a little bit more mature from our high school days, (or we should be anyways). We don't dwell on the friendships lost and instead, we look forward to the new people that we will meet.

College is also the time where you may discover people that you will want to hold on to as friends for the rest of your life. Who remembers those friends of yours, that help you deal with the stress of finals or new relationships! I bet they are still in your inner circle today.

And these types of friends are where distance and age make no difference where they are. When you reconnect, it's like being with them like it was yesterday!

Friends You Meet At Work — Having work friends can definitely make you happier on the job. After all, the average person works 40+ hours and chances are, you spend more time with your colleagues than your friends and family each week. And make no mistake, you can make lasting friendships with those you have worked with throughout your career years.

But… you must be mindful. Your co-workers and/or clients need to 'earn' the right to be a true friend. Remember one of the four traits of true friendship – trustworthiness? You will know with time, who you can trust and who you want to include in your life.

Friendships in Later Life — As we age 'gracefully' as I say since I am… the older generation has the luxury of being more selective of who their true friends are. Yes, we have longtime friends from childhood all the way thru college and career. But because 'time is more precious' in these formidable years, we tend to gravitate to those who are 'authentic' and who makes one feel special and important. In fact, it's common that many older adults have just as many friends of the younger generation as they do of their own age group.

In this regard, true friendship along these lines are more 'give and take' of imparting knowledge and wisdom and experiencing the 'freshness and energy' of youth. Cross-generational friendships can be just as every bit rewarding as same-aged friends.

The World Wide Web — I would be totally amiss if I didn't include the impact of the evolution of technology involving the creation of new and dynamic type relationships. In fact, one may never leave the boundaries of their state, let alone their country, and become international friends with anyone in the world today.

I could write another blog on this subject, which I may. But let me tell you this as a professional blogger… I have not just made friends, but true friends, from Australia to Pakistan to South Africa to Algeria to Great Britain to Florida to even someone I didn't even know was living 15 miles from me!

And you know what! Friends are friends are friends. It makes no difference how one is created. They are all just as important in experiencing the happiness that comes along with it.

A friend is someone who doubles your fun

and divides your sorrow.

-Euripides

THE FRIENDSHIP - HAPPINESS LINK

So by now, it should be very clear how the value of friendship, especially true friendship, translates to being a more happier person. In fact, survey after survey found that when an individual becomes happy, the net effect can be measured up to three degrees. One person's happiness triggers a chain reaction that benefits not only their friends, but their friends' friends, and their friends' friends' friends.

Having Happy Friends Can and Will Make You Happy.

Beth Elkassih, Author

7 WAYS WHY FRIENDS MAKE US HAPPIER

The importance of friendship in our lives obviously should never be taken for granted. Besides, true benefits cannot be measured (who can calculate how much joy or happiness one has received from all the years from your childhood or college best friend)?

When researching for writing this blog, I read literally 'hours' of content. But per this website, **Happify Daily**, the following are seven of the best reasons why friends make us so happy and I couldn't agree more!

1. **The Happiest People are the Most Social**
2. **Happiness Is Contagious**
3. **Friends Cut Out the Small Talk—and That Makes Us Happy**
4. **We Turn to Friends When We're Stressed**
5. **Our Friends Helps Us Be Optimistic**
6. **Friendships Improve Our Health**
7. **Our Friends Help Us Live Longer**

IN SUMMARY, THE VALUE OF FRIENDSHIP IS INDEED HAPPINESS!

In conclusion, friendship is intentional. Friendship is the serendipitous interactions with those selected few that exudes a spark of friendship chemistry. Friendship allows us to reach our higher self of actualization. And most importantly, friendship **IS INDEED HAPPINESS!**

There is nothing more joyful than sharing laughter with

true friends.

-Beth Elkassih, Author

CHAPTER SEVEN
DISCOVERING YOUR LIFE'S GRAND PURPOSE
Discover Your Life's Grand Purpose & Double Your Happiness

Let's imagine for a moment that you already have discovered your grand purpose in life. Regardless of what timeline you may be on… can you picture how wonderful life would be if you are living it with passion and purpose?

Can you see yourself waking up each morning eager to face the new day? You're filled with passion, zest, and energy to make a positive difference in this world with your gifts, talents, skills, knowledge, and abilities, right?

Those who live with confidence of knowing their life's purpose are those who put their whole heart, soul and passion into making a difference for everyone.

-Beth Elkassih

Discover how you can find your life's purpose. For some of you, you may already be living your life's purpose, but did you know that life can pivot us around and we end up easily having multiple grand life purposes throughout our lifetime?

We shall explore the various meanings and nuances concerning exactly what finding your life's purpose actually is composed of. We shall also examine how it is so important to find your purpose in life and provide several life purpose examples so you can see the bigger picture.

Finally, I will show you how you can double your happiness with 5 simple ways to find your own unique and personal *'Grand Purpose in Life'*.

THE MEANING OF FINDING YOUR LIFE'S PURPOSE

The search for happiness and our life's purpose is hardwired in our DNA. It transcends age, gender, geography, vocation, and personal circumstances. But how do you achieve it?

In researching to find out the exact meaning of this often-used cliche, this is what I discovered:

According to **Jayne Stevenson**, author of the blog article, **'Here's Why You Keep On Resisting Your Life Purpose'** in which she discusses how one can get 'crystal clarity about passion and purpose', she summarizes it as:

Who you believe you are, how you relate to others, and how you engage with the world around you is directly aligned with your purpose.

-Jayne Stevenson

No matter what religion or culture or part of the world you come from, it is a universal fact and belief that every person on the planet has a life purpose.

In France, they call it, **Raison d'être**, which literally means the most important reason or the purpose for someone or something's existence or "reason for being".

In Hindu cultures, **Dharma** is known as the "right way of living" and "path of rightness'. It is the conventional explanation of life purpose. Going further **Dharma** is the regulator of change and the principle which remains constant while change occurs; but dharma itself does not change.

The Japanese call it **Ikigai**, "our reason for living; meaning for life; what makes life worth living". **Ikigai** is all about finding joy in life through purpose. In other words, your ikigai is what gets you up every morning and keeps you going.

And for those of us who associate themselves being devout believers of one of the three **Abrahamic Religions (Judaism, Christianity and Islam)**, our religious belief plays a vital role in how we feel our life's purpose is directed. The relationship with **God/Allah** is interwoven into what our 'divine purpose/intention' in life is in regards to using the 'talents' or 'gifts' provided to us by **God/Allah** and using these determined strengths in helping others during our lifetime and how we treat our family, friends and strangers.

Today, we use the terms passion, purpose and life purpose interchangeably. Advice to live your passion, purpose or life purpose is pitched at you by friends, authors, celebrities, and meme makers.

The popular meaning is that passion, purpose and life purpose are emotionally based. The popular advice is that your most powerful emotions should be the guiding star that manifests your clear path forward. But is it?

LIFE PURPOSE EXAMPLES

To help our journey in determining what our own life purpose may take the form of, let's look at some thought-provoking examples to see if any resonates with you. I say, "your life purpose isn't determined by your 'brain', it is determined by your 'heart'".

Although everyone is different, there are common threads that bind a life with purpose.

- Do you live by your beliefs and values? Core beliefs and values influence our decisions, shape our day-to-day actions, and determine our short- and long-term priorities. You are known as a person of high integrity and have earned the trust and respect of others. You live with a clear conscience and end up spending more time listening to your inner voice than being influenced by others.

- Do you feel content? Living a life on purpose for you is possessing an inner peace. You're satisfied with what you have and who you are. Many mothers feel this way. Their purpose in life may simply be the best mom and parents to their children.

- Do you set priorities? People who live a life of purpose identify those activities that matter most to them and spend the majority of their time and effort in those areas. Otherwise, it's too easy to drift away in the currents of life. As **Annie Dillard**, the author, once said, "How we spend our days is, of course, how we spend our lives."

- Are you one to follow your passion? Earlier we spoke of those who live with passion where it is a delight just to wake up every morning and begin each day pursuing your goals and dreams intentionally. Like James Dean, the actor, once said, "Dream as if you'll live forever. Live as if you'll die today."

- Do you know how to achieve balance? Are you one of those people who put your heart and soul into your chosen career and who easily build relationships with friends and family? To achieve balance in your life, these people have mastered the art of understanding the importance of setting aside time to satisfy both their personal needs as well. Achieving balance means living up to one's potential in all facets of life

- Do you see yourself making a difference in the world? Or perhaps making a meaningful difference in someone else's life. You do things for others without expectation of personal gain, serve as exemplary role models, and gain as much satisfaction in witnessing the success of others as well as your own.

- Do you live in the moment? People who live a life of purpose cherish every moment and seek to live life without regret. They take joy in the experiences that life gives and don't worry about keeping score.

WHY IS IT IMPORTANT TO FIND YOUR PURPOSE IN LIFE?

Why is it so important to find our purpose in life? Well, I don't know about you, but for me, I don't want to be a bystander at the sidelines watching everybody have a satisfying and fulfilling life while I just 'exist day to day'! Do you? What joy is that? We all want to achieve happiness and fulfillment in our lives. It's built-in our DNA to have meaning in our lives and stand for something, right?

> ### *Without purpose, we surrender to living just a mediocre and average life...*
> ### *-Beth Elkassih*

Did you know that when you are living a life on purpose, it can truly be life transformational? Here are seven compelling reasons to make the effort and do your own self-journey into determining your 'Grand Purpose in Life'.

1. **It gives meaning to your life.** Finding your life purpose creates a sense of meaning in your life. You know what you love to do, what you are good at, and how you can contribute to the world.

2. **It provides a sense of place.** Finding a sense of meaning to life gives you a sense of place. When you have found your purpose, it is easier to know where you belong.

3. **It provides a greater ability in making choices.** When you know your life purpose you are more easily able to exercise choice in each moment of your life. You know better whether a situation or person really fits in your life because you know why you are here and what you want to do.

4. **It provides a sense of 'self'.** Knowing your life purpose gives you a clearer sense of who you are. By connecting to your sense of purpose, it provides a clear 'destination' of where it is you're ultimately trying to achieve.

5. **It provides the ability to 'live with ease'.** It comes to no surprise would it, that knowing your purpose makes life easier. You know what to pay attention to and what is less important. You spend less time and energy caught up on the things that don't really matter or have value in your life.

6. **It helps you in becoming 'self-confident'.** When you know your life purpose you are more confident. You know you are here for a reason and that your contribution counts. You KNOW we ALL have a purpose, whether we have found it yet or not.

7. **It allows you to make an impact or a difference in the world around you.** Knowing your purpose allows you to have a much greater impact on the world. Find your purpose and help contribute to a better world.

SIMPLE 3 STEPS IN FINDING YOUR LIFE PURPOSE

Per **Simon T. Bailey's** article he wrote in **Success Magazine** October 8, 2018, **'What is My Purpose in Life'**, to help illuminate your path as you seek your purpose, he offers this 3-step exercise he describes in his book, **Release Your Brilliance**, to help you discover your purpose and then design your life around it:

1. ASK

Ask yourself, How can I use my purpose to make a difference?—and your subconscious mind will open to the universe and its possibilities.

2. SEEK

Actively look for answers to how you can use your purpose each day. Look for the path that you're supposed to take. Do your research. Understand that you may have to follow a lot of rabbit trails, some of which will take you to dead ends. That's OK; it's all part of the process.

3. KNOCK

And keep knocking. Every single day takes one small step that moves you in the direction of your purpose. Write down your goal, then break down into smaller goals, and then even further into small, actionable steps. I promise you, these will add up quickly.

Remember this...

It only takes a 'moment' to change your life!

-Beth Elkassih

ADDITIONAL 5 LIFE-CHANGING STEPS TO FIND YOUR LIFE'S GRAND PURPOSE AND DOUBLE YOUR HAPPINESS!

So, are you still having trouble determining what your own personal life's grand purpose is? Let me empower you by giving you the tools you need in order to find YOUR Life's Grand Purpose.

Allow me to put some practicality in your search. I promise you, if you follow these five steps purposely and consciously every single day for a minimum of 21 consecutive days, I guarantee you will wake up in the not-too-distant future and find yourself with a serendipity 'new feeling of life' eager to face the new day.

You shall be filled with passion, zest, and energy to make a positive difference in this world with your gifts, talents, skills, knowledge and abilities right? And most importantly, you will experience a level of happiness you've never felt before and begin to REALLY live your life with intention and purpose each day.

1. **Start a Journal**: Do a life audit and record your findings. Find out what you are dissatisfied with and what brings you joy. It's important to record what you are feeling doing particular activities. Decide what you want to stop doing and what you would like to pursue.

2. **Dream Big:** Keep on writing in this journal... do some major brainstorming sessions and write what comes to your 'heart'! Ask yourself 'if this was your last month on earth what would you like to spend your time doing'? Or who with? (You get the picture, right!)

3. **Create a Vision Board:** A vision board helps you narrow down your desires through the power of choice. This tool helps you invest the time and energy to visualize your future and consistently reminds you of your life goals.

4. **Write your Life Purpose Statement:** Put down in words the true work you are here to do: the cause you will pursue, the problem you will devote your life to fixing. It states the highest, purest aim of your life. And once

you have finished writing this out, write it prominently in your journal and why not print it out on colorful paper and post it on your mirror in your bathroom to read every-single-day!

5. **Live in Joy and Happiness: Jack Canfield**, says you should do a 'Joy Review'! What makes you joyful? Go back to those life experiences and recall what you were doing at that time to experience that joy! And while you're at it, do a 'Happiness Review'!

IN SUMMARY

Now go out there and live your Life's Grand Purpose. And once you do, you will experience a level of happiness you will never allow to leave you again! Live again! Love Life!

We each have our own unique passion and purpose in

life... Have you discovered yours?

-Beth Elkassih, Author

CHAPTER EIGHT

THE POWER OF FORGIVENESS CAN BE A LIFE CHANGER!

Learn the Power of Forgiveness and Become a Happier Person

More than likely, we all have had someone who has wronged us in the past and caused much pain and anguish. It's hard to just simply forgive and forget. In fact, I don't think anyone forgets, especially if the incident was quite emotionally painful.

I will show you the true power of forgiveness and provide you with ways to learn to move on and bring back joy and happiness into your life. We will explore what is forgiveness and why it is so important to come to terms with it and the best methods of handling it.

Hopefully, by the end of this chapter, you shall be in a position to not only effectively forgive someone (and perhaps even yourself), but also see that it truly can be a life changer! And you will be rewarded with many blessings in return!

"TO ERR IS HUMAN, TO FORGIVE IS DIVINE"

Alexander Pope wrote those wise words. In the poem, **An Essay on Criticism, Part II, 1711, Pope** explains that, while anyone can make a mistake, we should aspire to do as God does, that is, show mercy and forgive sinners.

So what is forgiveness exactly and why is it so important? Forgiveness itself is actually the result of one forgiving another. More specifically forgiveness is a mental and/or spiritual process of acknowledging and 'letting go' of past sins committed against us.

Forgiveness is a 'choice' to let go of hanging on to grudges or bitterness and in the process, dealing with the 'hurt' in a positive way. We can never truly forgive, unless we learn to forgive our own self and use the power of 'love' when forgiving.

Forgiveness is for our own happiness and personal growth. The importance of the act of forgiving means you value yourself and your well-being first and foremost. Read this next quote and you will see the power that forgiveness has for you!

CAN YOU REALLY FORGIVE AND FORGET?

So you see, when you are forgiving, the power belongs to 'you'! Forgiveness frees us to live in the present. But let's talk about forgiving and forgetting. Can one really, honestly do that?

While it sounds good in 'theory', the reality is one shouldn't have to forget. Forgiving someone is not giving them a pardon for the wrong or hurt they caused. Forgiving is the ability to allow 'ourselves' to no longer be stuck and move on with our lives.

Sure, in time, memories will dull and the pain and hurt does indeed slowly heal. So I applaud those who can actually forget but I want to point out 4 reasons why I believe we shouldn't have to forget.

FOUR REASONS WHY SOMETIMES IT'S OKAY NOT TO FORGET WHEN FORGIVING SOMEONE

1. Forgiveness allows us to learn from past experiences. Perhaps there is a lesson to be learned. We need to be mindful of the lesson, and learn to move on and forward. This may mean putting distance between the person who hurt us.

2. Forgiveness protects our emotional health and well-being. I don't know about you, but for me, it simply just takes 'too much energy' to sustain being angry or upset at someone. Forgiveness replaces this negative energy with positivity and brings us back to happiness and joy.

3. Believe it or not, but forgiveness can also end up strengthening our relationships. All relationships can be restored, not despite what happened in the past but because of it. The act of forgiving can strengthen people's commitment to a healthy relationship if both are committed to doing so.

4. By not forgetting, we protect ourselves from being a victim of the same offense again. It's important to remember what happened to us in order for us to avoid letting it happen again.

Forgiveness liberates the soul!

-Nelson Mandela, Statesman

HEAR WHAT NELSON MANDELA HAS TO SAY ABOUT FORGIVENESS

Everyone knows that the word 'forgiveness' is synonymous with **Nelson Mandela** and how he lived his life. He will be remembered to have lived and died, loving and forgiving.

In 1969, while **Mandela** was in prison, he wrote "The threat of death evoked no desire in me to play the role of martyr.'

His famous quote, "Forgiveness liberates the soul, it removes fear," is such a powerful weapon. It is this forgiveness towards his nation's wrongdoers that he used as a weapon against the oppressive apartheid regime. His forgiveness of his enemies was truly life changing. This enabled the transformation of relationships, positive change and peace in his beloved country, South Africa.

And while we may never rise to the level of the **Honorable Mandela**, we all can learn proper, healthy steps to forgiveness.

To forgive is one of the greatest gifts of love a person

can give to one another.

-Beth Elkassih, Author

STEPS TO TRUE FORGIVENESS

- First and foremost, give yourself the needed time to cool off and reflec on everything that transpired. And there's no shame in letting it out... cry scream, vent... whatever you need to do.

- As hard as it may seem, learn to accept the person's apology. It take courage to admit when one is wrong. And by acceptance, you're closer t forgiveness and ultimately being happy again.

- Now's not the time to be timid. Let the person know exactly how you feel

- Show compassion. Think of all the good things that this person or frien did for you in the past.

- Reflect – did you ever wronged that person yourself in the past? Do yo need to make amends yourself?

- Consider the grand scheme of things—is there a lesson to be learned?

- If this relationship is meaningful to you, try to rebuild trust.

The day to forgive is everyday.

-Beth Elkassih

THE MOST POWERFUL EMOTION OF THEM ALL IN FORGIVENESS – LOVE

If you want to experience good health, happiness and joy in a balanced life, you have to make use of the power of forgiveness! And just as important, if one can also have unconditional love in the act of forgiveness, this truly will be a life changer.

Forgiveness and unconditional love is an art that takes time to learn. But when you learn how, the true Power of Forgiveness takes on a divine elevation and can and is a life changer.

IN CONCLUSION – ARE YOU READY TO FORGIVE?

I would be in total amiss if I didn't include what I feel is a very important component of the **"Power of Forgiveness"**. In fact, I would be willing to go on the record and state that 99% of those reading this blog are invested spiritually with their own individual faith and beliefs.

The concept of forgiveness might differ, but it still calls for love and a pure heart. For in my mind, the ultimate 'divine power of forgiveness' is provided to us in the unconditional love of **God/Allah**, etc. with the act of praying or meditating daily. And when you do this, forgiveness truly becomes life changing. Blessings to all!

CHAPTER NINE

MASTER THE ART OF GRATITUDE WITH THESE 15 TIPS

Mastering the Art of Gratitude

Discover how to master the art of gratitude with these 15 creative and innovative tips. Gratitude is widely known as a thankful appreciation for what an individual receives from another individual. But gratitude goes beyond the enlightenment of appreciation to God and/or a higher being. It can be life changing.

If you would like to find out what gratitude is, why the practice of gratitude is important and the benefits of gratitude, this post is for you. We shall also discuss these 15 best gratitude activities along with examples and the best ways to practice gratitude. By the end of this chapter, you will be well equipped to become a better and happier person.

THE POWER OF SAYING 'THANK YOU'!

We must realize the power of thank you is limitless. In fact, the more we find things to be thankful about, whether huge or even particularly small, then the more growth and well-being will flood into our lives.

The 'poor me' consciousness simply creates a culture of pessimism and negativity, a culture that overshadows our positive state of being. Whereas the vast vocabulary and the colorful language of thank you creates positivity and a real appreciation of things that are so easily overlooked. Thank you helps us to savor life and find beauty and truth, it helps us discover our true nature, abilities and talents.

Thank you stokes the fire of creativity and introduces us to higher levels of awareness and consciousness. The thank-you process motivates us to act because the appreciation that it produces gives us real power. It is a power that inspires, a power that rejoices more and complains less, a power that realizes our lives are dictated most of all by what thoughts we generate in our minds.

If you want more joy into your life, then master the art of gratitude.
-Beth Elkassih

WHAT IS GRATITUDE?

The Latin word known as 'gratia' is where the word gratitude originated. 'Gratia' means grace, graciousness, or gratefulness. Gratitude is also associated with sincere appreciation from receiving a kind gesture from someone.

When you have gratitude in your life, you begin to realize all the goodness in your life and the goodness of other people in turn. As a result, gratitude also helps people connect to something larger than themselves as individuals — whether to other people, nature, or a higher power.

Greater happiness within oneself is also associated with gratitude as well as having a healthy dose of well-being.

WHY IS THE PRACTICE OF GRATITUDE IMPORTANT

Few things in life are as important to our well-being and happiness as gratefulness and the practice of gratitude.

-Beth Elkassih, Author

Everyone wants to experience more happiness and emotional well-being. In today's world, it has received more popularity in both psychological research and scientific studies in the nature and practice of gratitude.

Researchers like **Martin Seligman, Robert Emmons, and Michael McCullough** have come up with some impressive insights which should be highly noted. Their findings include:

Our thoughts can actually trigger physiological changes in our body that affects our mental and physical health.

- If you increase your positive thoughts, like gratitude, you can increase your subjective sense of well-being as well.

- Practicing gratitude also can be measured objectively as it is observed that physical health benefits include fewer symptoms of illness and increased immune functioning as a result.

A study from the **National Institutes of Health (NIH)** examined blood flow in various brain regions while subjects summoned up feelings of gratitude.

Higher levels of activity in the hypothalamus were found in subjects who showed more gratitude overall.

Furthermore, these higher levels of activity include an array of essential bodily functions, including eating, drinking and sleeping. It also has a huge influence on your metabolism and stress levels.

Feelings of gratitude directly activated brain regions are also associated with the neuro-transmitter dopamine, the 'feel-good' chemical released when emotions of happiness are experienced.

THE BENEFITS OF GRATITUDE LEAD YOU TO A BETTER & HAPPIER LIFE

- Gratitude improves physical and mental health
- Gratitude improves self-esteem
- Gratitude enhances empathy & reduces negative emotions
- Gratitude improves our quality of sleep
- Gratitude makes people like us more
- Gratitude strengthens our emotion

- Gratitude leads to a positive attitude

- Gratitude enables us to be much happier in life

- Gratitude brings us much joy and blessings

MASTER THE ART OF GRATITUDE WITH THESE 15 TIPS

Want to start being a better and happier person? Let's get proactive and get inspired in mastering the art of gratitude with these 15 tips!

TIP 1: GRATITUDE JOURNALING

TIP 2: WRITE THANK-YOU NOTES

TIP 3: THANK-YOU NOTES VIA SOCIAL MEDIA

TIP 4: CREATE A GRATITUDE GARDEN

TIP 5: GRATITUDE WALKS

TIP 6: CREATE A GRATITUDE TREE

TIP 7: CREATE A GRATITUDE JAR

TIP 8: GIVE GRATITUDE FLOWERS

TIP 9: CREATE A GRATITUDE ROCK

TIP 10: CREATE A GRATITUDE BOX

TIP 11: READ BOOKS ABOUT GRATITUDE

TIP 12: RESPOND WITH GRATITUDE AND DONATE

TIP 13: CREATE AN INSPIRING THANKFUL WINDOW

TIP 14: CREATE A GRATITUDE COLLAGE

TIP 15: CREATE YOUR OWN GRATITUDE MINDSET

Gratitude Turns What We Have Into Enough.

-Hindu Saying

IN CONCLUSION...

In conclusion, **Melody Beattie** says it best: "Gratitude unlocks the fullness of life". It turns what we have into enough, and more. It turns denial into acceptance, chaos to order, and confusion to clarity. It can turn a meal into a feast, a house into a home, a stranger into a friend. Gratitude makes sense of our past, brings peace for today and creates a vision for tomorrow.

You were also reminded that the definition of what gratitude truly is, why the practice of gratitude is so important and described the many benefits that gratitude provides.

15 Tips were shared on how to 'master the art of gratitude' with thought-provoking activities for both children and adults alike.

For additional motivation, I leave you with this incredible thought-provoking comment from **Denzel Washington**.

Say thank you in advance for what's already yours.

-Denzel Washington

CHAPTER TEN

THE AWESOME HEALING POWER OF JOURNALING

Want to Change Your Life? Learn This One Habit... Journal!

Want to change your life? Learn this one habit – journal! Master the awesome power of journaling. Journaling is a trending subject that has captured both the world and the internet by storm!

Journaling is so much more than putting 'pen to paper'! Did you know that there are awesome healing powers of journaling as well? I'm not only going to explain in-depth what exactly journaling is but also the powerful health benefits one receives by engaging in this daily exercise.

We will then spend some time looking into a couple of scientific studies showing the powerful healing side of journaling as well. We shall learn how journaling can help therapeutically heal and help us 'cope' with depression, anxiety and stress. In addition, we shall explore how one can heal through journaling even in cases of loss or grief.

So who needs to change their life or learn how to heal from depression, anxiety or stress? Let's begin, shall we...

Journal writing becomes a journey into your soul.

-Beth Elkassih

SO WHAT IS THIS 'SELF-CARE' MOVEMENT KNOWN AS JOURNALING ANYWAYS?!?

Today one can go to the internet and google the word 'journal' and there are so many different types of journals available. There are 'dream journals', 'workout journals', bullet journals (we'll get into this in a moment…), 'food journals', 'travel journals', 'gratitude journals' and the list goes on and on. All with the goal in mind of tracking our progress and thoughts in doing-so. Why all the fuss?

Simply stated, they work. And not only that, it's one of the cheapest self-care habits one can learn easily. All it takes is just a sheet of paper and a pen or pencil!

Journaling has been proven to provide positive well-being and significant health benefits including therapeutic healing from mental health issues as well as loss and grief.

Great Thinkers All Kept Journals!

So for those of you who think 'journaling' is something trivial and don't feel as if it's for you, think again! Would it surprise you to know that throughout our history, great men and women have been known for keeping a journal?

Journaling (or keeping letters or diaries) is an ancient tradition, one that dates back to at least 10th century Japan. As stated earlier, successful people and visionaries throughout history have kept journals. These include the likes of **Albert Einstein, Benjamin Franklin, Leonardo da Vinci, Maya Angelou and Nicola Tesla,** to name just a few.

No one can argue the extraordinary contributions to humanity each has done. And they all relied on the one 'powerful and awesome habit known as journaling' whose unique insights and perspectives on the world around them have resonated for generations.

Life-Changing Benefits of Journals Discovered

Lena Schmidt of The Chopra Center, states: "Writing down your thoughts, dreams, feelings, and ideas is a healthy and beneficial practice for overall wellness. Writing helps get to the heart of the matter by getting whatever you're dealing with off your mind and onto the page. Writing about the pain of heartbreak, the confusing feelings that arise after an argument, or the mess of your life after a big transition helps make those feelings real."

LIST OF MAJOR LIFE-CHANGING BENEFITS DERIVED BY JOURNALING

Here are some of the more important life-changing benefits that I myself have found to be true:

- Journaling Makes You Smarter
- Journaling Reduces Your Stress Levels
- Journaling Makes You Nicer ... and More Grateful
- Journaling Keeps You More Focused

- Journaling Organizes Your Thoughts

- Journaling Helps Turn Your Dreams Into Goals

- Journaling Provides Well-Being for your Mind and Spirit.

List of Benefits From the Actual Process of 'Writing'

Benefits are not just derived from journaling in of itself. Did you know that there re even significant health benefits to the act of 'writing' itself? Let's take a look... Keep a daily journal of your dreams, goals and accomplishments.

Journaling allows one to record life's most memorable

moments.

-Beth Elkassih

SCIENTIFIC STUDIES PROVING THE POWERFUL AWESOME HEALING POWERS OF JOURNALING

- Writing Improves Blood Pressure Levels

- Writing Improves Mood

- Writing Increases Feelings of Well-Being

- Writing Increases our Immune System

- Writing Improves our Memory

Maud Percell, LCSW, who penned the article "The Health Benefits c Journaling, states: There is increasing evidence to support the notion tha journaling has a positive impact on physical well-being. "

In fact, **James Pennebaker**, psychologist and researcher from th **University of Texas at Austin** argues that by engaging in regular journaling, strengthens immune cells, called T-lymphocytes.

Other research indicates that journaling decreases the symptoms of asthm and rheumatoid arthritis. Pennebaker also believes that writing about stressfu events helps you come to terms with them, acting as a stress management too thus reducing the impact of these stressors on your physical health.

In another scientific research program from the **University of Rochest Medical Center,** journaling was determined to be a healthy outlet and a positiv coping mechanism for helping people face overwhelming emotions. Likewise journaling also has been proven that it has far-reaching healing benefits in regarc to mental health as well.

Here are five 'mental health' benefits that the **University of Rochest Medical Center** reports:

1.   Helps Manages and Reduces Depression and Anxiety.

2.   Minimizes Everyday Stress.

3.   Helps Prioritizes Fears and Concerns.

4.   Provides Opportunities for Recognizing Triggers.

5.   Allows space for positive encouragement and self-talk.

Journaling is a self-reflection which is worth listening to any time we need to be reminded.

-Beth Elkassih

The Awesome Healing Power of Journaling During the Grieving Process

One of the most significant healing powers that journaling provides is for those following the loss of a loved one.

If you are on a healing journey through loss, grief, addiction, or are genuinely interested in personal growth, expressive writing is a beneficial beginning toward improving your emotional well-being.

The Awesome Power of Journaling for Mental Health

I know earlier we mentioned some of the journaling benefits in regards to depression, anxiety and stress. By keeping a special therapy journal dedicated to assisting you on your therapeutic healing journey, you can increase awareness and insight.

When faced with a particularly emotional or challenging situation, journal writing can also be used as a tool for stress management to reset or de-stress following these types of situations.

Want to stop negative thoughts from crowding your mind? It's been found that writing can also be used to interrupt the negative thought patterns and help 'rewire' the brain to find helpful solutions. According to the **Center for Journal Therapy**, an education and training center whose mission is "to make the healing art and science of journal writing accessible to all who desire self-directed change," journaling is a healthy therapeutic tool for healing, growth, and change.

Let's find out what their therapy journal training center suggests and offers to their client journalers.

- Keep it Private.
- Meditate Before You Write.
- Date Each Entry.
- Keep and Re-Read What You Write.
- Write Quickly.
- Write Without Editing or Censoring Yourself.
- Give Yourself Permission to Tell Yourself the Truth
- Write Naturally in a Way That Works Best for You.

SO WHAT DO I WRITE ABOUT???

First and foremost, there are simply 'no rules' when it comes to journaling. It truly is just 'pen and paper' and the possibilities are endless. Some people use 'journal prompts' to help them get started. But all you need to do is just sit quietly and let your creative juices flow through you.

You will find that through time and practicing putting your 'private thoughts' on paper, that it will become easier for you.

Here are some of the more popular 'journal prompts' taken from **The Chopra Center** which you can use to help you in your initial journal writing routine:

- What would you do if you knew you could not fail?

- Write a love letter to the world.

- If I'm really honest. . .

- What I do every day matters more than what I do once in a while, so today I. . .

- Imagine you've got a whole day to do everything you love. What would this blissful day look like?

- I drank a sunset. . .

- How are you feeling right now?

- I am. . .

- I feel. . .

- I do. . .

- I love. . .

- I speak. . .

- I see. . .

- I understand. . .

- What won't let you be? What imbalances can you identify in your life?

- What causes fear to arise when you think about the future? What would you do should what you fear come to be?

- What causes happiness to arise when you think about the future? What could you do to create more happiness in your life as you are living it right now?

- I wonder. . .

- The best adventure I ever had began when. . .

- If I wait to be ready, I'll never. . .

There are no rules when it comes to journaling.

-Beth Elkassih, Author

99

CHAPTER ELEVEN

LIFE ISSUES - ARE YOU LIVING OR ARE YOU JUST EXISTING?

LIVING VERSUS EXISTING!

Are you living or are you just existing?! Are you at the end of your rope nd wondering what is going on with you?

This article is a very important subject, especially in light of the current ontinuation of this 2020 Covid pandemic. Especially now when we find most of urselves stuck in our houses and experiencing week after week of lockdown and eing mindful of social distancing. (It's quite annoying, right!...)

In fact, how many of you are at the breaking point of just saying 'I just on't care anymore and find yourself just simply 'existing' day to day to just get y? You CAN enjoy life again. Let's discover how.

But first, let's examine what living versus existing really is. According to aul Mc*Gregor,* **who is a mental health blogger himself, states:**

"Living is taking life as it comes, embracing it and doing as much s you can to feel fulfilled. Existing is a long survival. Living is choosing appiness, it's choosing to live. Existing is you being here physically, but 'oing what you have to do to get through the day." – **Paul McGregor**

Does any of this resonate with you? I have to admit, it definitely is easy to :e why many of us are struggling right now because of this insidious pandemic. appears to me maybe, just maybe, many of us are actually experiencing a little it of both! We are doing what we have to do to get through the day, right?

HAVE YOU TEMPORARILY LOST YOUR SPARKLE?

But let me re-ask the question…

Are you living, or are you merely existing?

Ponder this for a moment or two.

Do you feel you are currently living a life of fulfillment and happiness? C perhaps you feel you are but now, it's more of a passive experience rather tha feeling that enthusiasm, passion and engagement of your life you once had.

Existing is a trap we easily fall into with the same ole, same 'ole dai routine of going through our day.

Uncertainty about the future definitely puts a 'spin' which gives everythin else a sort of pointless edge.

ANHEDONIA – REDUCED ABILITY TO FEEL PLEASURE…

Would it surprise you that there is a medical term associated with th feeling of just 'existing'?! **Anhedonia**_is an inability or reduced ability to fe pleasure, enjoyment, and engagement with life. It also includes reduced motivatio to do things plus that all too familiar attitude of just not caring about anythin Nothing feels good or brings you fulfillment.

But here's the deal… Life is not just about being alive. There's a bi difference. It's not merely breathing and going through the 'motion' of dai activities and chores.

To live doesn't mean you're alive. We're all born and gifted with life. Bu all too often we get caught up in false expectations. We truly forget how to liv our lives with freedom and passion.

To live life to the fullest means waking up every morning with purpose… not rolling out of bed simply because you have to!

Living life is chasing and fulfilling your dreams and doing whatever it takes to achieve them. Not giving up on them because of excuses.

Living life is also about being grateful for everything you have. And not to have feelings of unworthiness or trying to find what you haven't got.

And finally, **living life** is about embracing change and growth. To fully enjoy every moment in our life as it comes to us.

Remember this. It only takes a moment to change the course of your life… It's all in your control.

-Beth Elkassih, Author

ARE YOU IN CONTROL OF YOUR LIFE?

Have you ever wondered how much control you have over your life? It all starts with you! Yes, you have to know the difference between those things or situations that you cannot control (like the pandemic).

Think about it. Are you controlled instead by your emotions being 'all over the place'? Or are you controlled by your ego, by your job title or by the opinions of others? Or the big one — are you controlled by fear?

Existing is fruitless and it just passes the survival of time. Let me tell you something…

It only takes a moment to change the course of your life. A moment. Do you know how significant this statement is?

"It only takes a moment to change the course of your life."

Living is choosing happiness, it's choosing to live.

Let's take a step further… I want you to repeat this next statement OUT LOUD to yourself and as many times as you need to. Say it. Say it again louder. Say it until you believe it!

"It only takes a moment to change the course of MY LIFE."

Feels good, doesn't it? Are you ready to stop 'existing' and start living the life you're meant to live? Let me remind you of something… it's your undeniable birthright to live the life you were 'created' to live.

HOW YOU CAN REBOOT AND START
LIVING LIFE AGAIN

You're all familiar with the term, 'reboot', right? Rebooting is a computer technical troubleshooting method. Basically, when your computer is giving you trouble—for example, a program locks up or is simply not responding–you shut it down and restart it.

Likewise, when we find ourselves just 'existing' and/or lost our direction in pursuing our passions and enjoying all life's precious moments, we need to do a 'reboot', shut down and restart.

ARE YOU LIVING LIFE TO THE FULLEST YET?

Regardless of where you're coming from, you can get a fresh start on your life by figuring out where you want to go. Take a look at these four steps detailed below and see how many you can include in your life.

1. GAIN A FRESH PERSPECTIVE

You've got to take a step back and gain a fresh perspective on just where you are and determine where you want to go. Being able to control how you look at things is the key to learning how to start over and creating a fresh start.

In fact, shaping your perception is so powerful that just a small change in perspective can completely change everything, from your motivation and outlook, to your self-esteem and confidence.

2. DEFINE YOUR PERSONAL VALUES OR YOUR MORAL COMPASS

If you have a desire to reboot your life, it may be because you don't feel like you are living according to your principles. Personal values are the beliefs, opinions, and ideas that drive your decision-making and serve as a foundation for your life. To many people, this includes our devout religious beliefs.

3. ENVISION THE BEST VERSION OF YOURSELF

A visualization is a powerful tool you can use to clarify our desires and move us closer to what we really want from our life. Envision your best possible self. Spend some time imagining who you would like to be in 5, 10, or 15 years.

4. GET MOTIVATED AND PLAN OUT YOUR GOALS

Even if you have a good plan, it won't work unless you develop motivation and positive habits that will keep you on track. These habits can include goal setting, daily reflections, and perseverance.

FINAL THOUGHTS

So, let me make it simple for you. When you're ready to pull the trigger… to take that moment to change the trajectory of your life… the sequence is as follows:

1) That magical moment – when you take control of your life and seize the moment to change your life and start living again your hopes and dreams.

2) Shut down and forgive yourself for the past… When you shut down, you're clearing out all the 'clutter' in your past to move forward. To start with a clean slate.

3) Restart living life again! This is that indescribable moment of feeling immediate joy and happiness **KNOWING** you're not only back on the right path, but **KNOWING** that you're in total control of what you want from your life, the choices in front of you to become the best person you can become!

So I again ask you… *Are you living or are you just existing!?!*

CHAPTER TWELVE

10 POWERFUL TIPS IN OVERCOMING ANXIETY ATTACKS!

IS IT JUST NERVES OR IS IT JUST ANXIETY

Is it just nerves or is it just anxiety that you suffer with? This chapter will describe '10 powerful tips in overcoming anxiety attacks, or more specifically, social anxiety.' All of us from time to time have experienced anxiety with our nerves acting up when confronted with social situations. Who hasn't felt this way when preparing for a big speech or a job interview or even going out on a date?

We shall explore what exactly social anxiety is and the myths and misconceptions associated with it. We will also look at the symptoms and what situations usually trigger an anxiety or panic attack.

Then, 10 powerful tips on overcoming social anxiety using cognitive behavior strategies will be conveyed so that the next time you find yourself with sweaty palms, increased breathing, and 'butterflies', you will be well prepared on knowing what to do.

WHAT IS SOCIAL ANXIETY EXACTLY?

According to **Mental Health of America**, social anxiety, also known as SAD (Social Anxiety Disorder) is an anxiety disorder characterized by extreme fear or anxiety in one or more social settings. Going to a party or even having a one-on-one conversation with a new person can result in increased heart rate, sweating, and racing thoughts for someone with social anxiety.

When social anxiety gets significant, it's common for individuals to isolate themselves and feel very alone. Oftentimes, the overwhelming feeling of 'dread' makes the one who is suffering hard to function in daily life. And taken to extremes, they may regularly avoid the 'anxiety-inducing' situations altogether leading to further isolation from family and friends.

HOW COMMON IS SOCIAL ANXIETY WORLDWIDE?

It is estimated that a staggering 264 million people worldwide suffer from this condition as of 2017. The prevalence of anxiety disorders across the world varies from 2.5 to 7 % by country. Is it any surprise that anxiety is considered to be the most prevalent mental health condition in our society today?

In fact, in the United States alone, 40 million people suffer from social anxiety._Social anxiety can affect both men and women, with women slightly leading in the statistical data of 60%. It does not discriminate. Several well-known world leaders and celebrities struggle with this disorder as well.

Learn to live in the moment. Take the 'nuggets' of life experience from the past and turn them into wisdom for living in the present!

- Beth Elkassih

SYMPTOMS OF SOCIAL ANXIETY -- WHAT DOES IT FEEL LIKE

There are many symptoms associated with social anxiety. In fact, it affects each person differently depending upon the severity and of course, the situation at hand. I'm sure we can all relate to one or more in the following list:

- Rapid Heart Rate

- Blushing

- Sweating, especially the Palms

- Trembling

- Feeling Nauseated

- Having Butterflies in Your Stomach

- Dizziness and Lightheadedness

- Diarrhea

- Trouble Catching Your Breath

- Muscle Tension

- The Feeling Your Mind Going Blank

- The Feeling of your Stomach Tied Up in Knots

THE STRUGGLE IS REAL

There are several misconceptions concerning social anxiety. Those of us who suffer are so misunderstood and oftentimes, people are quick to judge and say 'we're just a basket case of drama'…

It manifests differently in each person. Try to put yourself in their shoes. They suffer from 'overthinking' or ruminating over worst-case scenarios.

It's not just about being stressed — it's the unknown factor. It's about being overwhelmed with a new situation never experienced before. The struggle is real and is magnified when we find ourselves spending too much time alone.

STAGE FRIGHT – PERFORMANCE ANXIETY

Let's take a moment and discuss another type of social anxiety, known as performance anxiety. Or should I say, 'stage fright'?

Many times when we feel anxiety, it can be in a situation experiencing heightened emotions or excitement. Especially when we personally experience something new. So social anxiety isn't necessarily triggered by a phobia of fear. It can easily be that we haven't had that particular experience in our life yet.

Nerves and anxiety in the stomach is the engine roar

before it soars!

-Unknown

One of the most well-known entertainers, **Barbra Steisand** developed overwhelming performance anxiety at the height of her career; for 27 years she refused to perform for the general public.

And yes, the iconic **Mark Zuckerberg**, founder of Facebook openly admits that he suffers from social anxiety. In fact, on his first real job interview, he found himself stuttering and sweating 'bullets'. Since then he has transformed from being socially awkward to a polished public figure. But even at the Senate Hearings in 2018, dealing with Facebook issues, he was under tremendous stress and experienced 'performance anxiety'.

MY OWN PERSONAL ANXIETY ATTACK!

When I made the decision to write about this topic, it was partly because I, myself, experienced this phenomenon while preparing for a new situation I had never faced before.

I just recently became a published author ('The Power of Unexpected Miracles') and a 'book-signing event' was set up. As the event approached, I noticed my anxiety levels were creeping up on me. I don't know why I started feeling the way I did. Public speaking was something I was already doing.

However, upon reflection, this was indeed a NEW situation. I never was an author before... I didn't know what to expect with this event! I allowed the 'fear of the unknown' to get to me. And yes, my friends, I was close to being very ill and the 'butterflies' just wouldn't go away! I was in fact, experiencing 'stage fright' or performance anxiety!

10 POWERFUL TIPS IN OVERCOMING ANXIETY ATTACKS!

1. **KNOW** that you CAN overcome this.

2. **STOP** overthinking it!

3. **REALIZE** people are too busy with their own issues. They really don't care as much as you think they do!

4. **STOP** feeling embarrassed – you're only human!

5. **LOOK** for the good in people – and remember this – more than likely you shall probably be among empathic people who have stood in your shoes!

6. **LEARN** to **BELIEVE** in yourself again. This is a confidence issue. You got this!

7. **DETERMINE** your triggers. What situations cause you the most stress? **LEARN** to quiet these thoughts and feelings.

8. **RESPOND**… don't react or give in to your anxiety.

9. **REACH OUT** to a trusted friend who allows you to vent and who can gently but firmly **REMIND** you to put everything in perspective and to breathe, reflect and reassure you things will be alright.

10. **PRAY and PRAY and PRAY** some more. Let God help you through this!

IN CONCLUSION

In conclusion, social anxiety is a real mental health condition and should be treated as such. This chapter presented 10 strategically powerful tips on how to overcome everyday anxiety attacks. More specifically, these tips are behavior modification techniques. These are great when getting over a singular 'anxiety attack' or if one just has a 'mild case' of anxiety.

That said, do KNOW that if YOU experience anxiety more severely or find that it persistently lasts for months or you find yourself becoming depressed as well, you need to seek professional medical treatment.

Most of the things you worry about actually NEVER happen. Stop worrying and Start Living!

-Beth Elkassih, Author

CHAPTER THIRTEEN

FINALLY TAKE CHARGE OF YOUR LIFE & START BELIEVING IN YOURSELF AGAIN!

TAKE CHARGE OF YOUR LIFE!

In this chapter, I am so anxious to present this life-changing and thought provoking article on how to finally take charge of your life and start believing in yourself again.

We shall discuss the signs of how you may have 'lost yourself' or have become disillusioned with your everyday status. We will ask tough questions about the current 'reality' of your life as it stands today and present thought-provoking strategies to propel you into necessary actions that have the potential to change your life for the better.

By the end of this blog article, I will encourage you and teach you how to eliminate self-doubt, how to take control, and take back your life. You will discover how to have faith in yourself, believe in yourself, regain your happiness, and find yourself again.

FEELING LOST OR 'EMPTY INSIDE'...

Do you find yourself lately feeling lost or empty inside? Like having gaping hole in your well-being and you just don't know how to close it up!?!

Do you feel unfulfilled with your job and wish you could be doing something you really love? And what about those of you who may be just going 'through the motions' of just getting through the day with the bare minimum of effort. Have you become complacent?

You are human after all and we all have experienced these types of feelings, albeit, some more than others, at various times of our life. The question becomes…. What do we do about it? How can we start believing in ourselves again, have faith in ourselves, and regain that confidence and happiness one needs to not only take charge of our life but start to begin reliving the life we were meant to live!

Can you relate to any of these questions? Yes, finding yourself again may seem impossible right now, but trust me, there is hope.

Do you want to know how to successfully know how to find yourself again? If you commit to doing so, you have the potential of radically transforming your life, finding happiness and joy again, and become the best version of yourself.

Find what makes you truly happy… not just 'happy enough', then you will experience pure joy.

-Beth Elkassih

HOW TO ELIMINATE SELF-DOUBT AND REGAIN CONFIDENCE

Discover how to eliminate self-doubt and live your best life. Falling out of touch with yourself happens when you buy into other ideas of what you are supposed to be or should be doing. Have you found yourself following what you think you are supposed to be doing rather than what you WANT to be doing? If so, you are not living your own life.

You need to learn to regroup and realize that only your true self can lead you in the right direction of happiness, confidence, regain passion and revalidate your life.

Here are 5 tips to learn how to eliminate self-doubt, regain your confidence and take charge of your life and lead a meaningful life:

1. **Rediscover what makes you YOU! What makes you tick!**
2. **Learn how to take better self-care of yourself!**
3. **Make time for the people and things that you love!**
4. **Start thinking outside the box and don't apologize if what you think isn't what the 'average Joe' thinks!**
5. **Stop second-guessing yourself! Trust your instincts!**

Your inner-self knows what your passions are. Call it intuition if you will! Your inner-self knows the right choices to make if you just learn to 'listen'.

Discover what life is trying to teach you and embrace it!

-Beth Elkassih

Mary Capino goes further in stating that when you hit what you think may be a breaking point, you shouldn't resist it, but embrace it. In fact, she says to walk right into it.

Often these moments are occurring precisely to illuminate what you're missing in your life, and what you deeply long for. When you learn to embrace rather than fight the lessons these challenging moments are trying to teach you, suddenly a new path becomes clearer and more possible than ever before.

THE MOST IMPORTANT RELATIONSHIP THAT YOU WILL EVER HAVE!

Did you know that the most important relationship that you will ever have is yourself?

When you finally start taking charge of your life and when you start believing in yourself again, it involves having a healthy relationship with yourself. Having a healthy relationship means that you have a stable self-concept. You learn to be comfortable 'within your own skin'. You learn that you don't need anyone's approval of others to feel whole.

Did you also know that it is scientifically proven that if you look up and smile your biggest grin possible, you can no longer feel depressed… You can no longer be angry… it's just not possible… The chemicals in your brain when looking up and simultaneously smiling will not allow you to be anything but happy! Do you know how incredible this statement is?

Per **Huffington Post, 'The Key to a Successful Relationship: Have One With Yourself First'**, studies have shown that people who put themselves first show self-interest without being selfish and are simply, much happier. When you feel good about yourself, it compliments every other relationship that you have.

Not only that, self-love is the best kind of love (outside of religious love/devotion of course). It allows one to connect to our soul's purpose and live the life that we want. Let me resonate this thought with you further by quoting the late, insightful Louise Hay:

Loving ourselves works miracles in our lives.

-Louise Hay

DO YOU BELIEVE THAT CHANGE IS POSSIBLE FOR YOU?

Let's face it. Life will always present us with challenges. There are times when we may find ourselves in the midst of a life crisis. Excuses hold us back from being the best we can be, from being honest with ourselves and living authentic lives.

Learn these 12 strategies and discover the power of greatness within you! Let's face it. Life can be difficult at times and it's nice to have some 'lifelines' in easy reach.

STRATEGIES ON HOW TO TAKE CHARGE AND TAKE BACK YOUR LIFE

- Take Responsibility, Then Accept It
- Take Note of Those You Admire and Don't Admire
- Live a Healthy Lifestyle
- Write In a Journal
- Ask Yourself Questions
- Do More of What You Love
- Get Out of Your Comfort Zone
- Pick Up Hobbies and Learn New Skills
- Forgive Yourself for Everything
- Embrace Spontaneity and Do Something Crazy or 'Out of the Box!'
- Live in the Moment

Life begins at the end of your comfort zone.

-Beth Elkassih, Author

START BELIEVING IN YOURSELF! DREAM BIG & MAKE GOALS BECOME REALITY ONCE AND FOR ALL!

If you want to learn how to find happiness, look inside of yoursel. Happiness is an inside job. It is the result of being present with ourselves.

Yes, personal growth isn't always fun. It's not a straightforward line process. There will be good days and not so good days. That's just how life work.

One of my favorite motivational speakers is the well-known **Ton Robbins**. I loved reading his book, **"Awaken The Giant Within"** where he tall about taking charge of your life. Here's the deal...

According to **Tony**, you must learn to take charge of your life an understand that many people give away their power to their boss, spous environment, external influences, and peer pressure from family and friends.

He goes on to say... "Whose life are you really living? Is it one of yo own making? Or is it one on another's making? Are you truly satisfied with the li that you are living? Look within, is this from you? Is this all that you are capab of becoming and achieving?"

You know and I know the answer is a resounding 'No!'... You know ve well deep inside of yourself that you can become more and ultimately achie more! Do you realize there are simply no limits as to what you can achieve!

You CAN become the person you truly want to be and achieve all that yo want to achieve!

Yes, I am here to remind you to take charge of your life again... You CA believe in yourself and you NEED to take action. And please, please, please... I NOT ever let anyone take control of your life!

It is YOUR life and you CAN live it in whatever way you choose to live it! Don't become a slave to someone else's dream, take control, have faith in yourself and allow yourself to be the architect of your own PERSONAL dreams.

Stop doubting your greatness and start reliving the

life you were born to live!

-Beth Elkassih

99

THE BIG TAKEAWAY!

So don't delay any longer! Begin the process of believing in yourself and **DREAM BIG** and make those goals become reality.

Take small steps, but dream big dreams. And remember:

FINALLY TAKE CHARGE OF YOUR LIFE AND START BELIEVING IN YOURSELF AGAIN!

CHAPTER FOURTEEN

BEYOND SADNESS - HELPING YOUR FRIENDS TO SMILE AGAIN!

I JUST WANT MY FRIEND TO SMILE AGAIN...

I am so excited to be able to present this next chapter, 'Beyond Sadness - Helping Your Friends Smile Again'. How many of us know a dear friend, perhaps even a couple or more who are currently struggling with sadness or depression?

One of the most dynamic and thoughtful things one can do is making the effort to make someone smile and brighten their day. It's nice to be nice.

It takes someone who really cares, who is authentic and is willing to put in the effort to make a genuine difference when trying to make someone happy.

This chapter, Beyond Sadness – Helping Your Friends Smile Back, will provide meaningful ways of how you can help your friends (or family) struggling with sadness and despair to find their way back to be able to smile again!

SHOW THEM YOU TRULY CARE!

I don't care how sad or depressed someone is, everyone wants to feel happier. Your friends want to know they are both appreciated and loved. Always – no matter what – greet them with a smile and make sure you call them by their name. Ask them how they are and that you are thinking of them.

Be emotionally supportive by letting them know you will always be there for them. And know that in times of grief, patience is a virtue.

Hugs are one of the most overlooked powerful gestures we can give to one another. It not only shows that you care, but they are truly healing. That said, it is both ***important and respectful*** to always ask first if it's okay to hug them. Some may not be ready for it or it's simply a cultural thing.

But do know this... just the mere act of 'asking' will make a strong impact on your friend. Try it and be prepared for a positive response!

BE IN THE PRESENT!

Let's try our best and get beyond their sadness and make that effort to get them to smile back again. One way to do this is by learning to be a good listener. Be in the present with them. And by all means, **PLEASE** put away your cell phone. This tells them when they're talking, that you value their thoughts and you're giving him or her the attention they deserve.

And please try your best to refrain from interrupting them. **ALWAYS** let them finish. This is one of the best ways to make people feel good about themselves. And who knows, perhaps you will learn why they feel the way they do that you didn't know beforehand.

And oh yes, LISTEN. It works.

REACH OUT!

With the modern technology of today, there's not a better time than to take advantage of using social media! You know and I know, we all like to hear that familiar **'ding'** announcing to us to let us know someone is sending a message. Call, text, **Facebook,** or even email your friend(s) and engage with them in meaningful conversation! And yes, as a second reminder, don't forget to address them by their name.

For some people, messaging via social media actually allows them to 'open up' more than they would have if in person. Not everyone, but for those who are somewhat introverted, this is an excellent option to help those who need this type of engagement to connect and have meaningful dialogue.

And remember, you know you're getting thru once you see that all too familiar **smiley face icon**!?

SURPRISE THEM!

When was the last time a friend surprised YOU? It was an instant pick-me-up wasn't it? And come on now, you know you had to be smiling when receiving it!

Flowers will never go out of style. Women love flowers but so do men and boys and girls! Plants, succulents or anything related to gardening are all ideal choices to make someone get their smile back!

And what about tickets?! Yes! They can be for a sporting event, theater, concert or even a comedy show! And with tickets, you're getting your friend up and out the door to engage in an activity that brings fun back into their life. Priceless...

HELP GET THEIR PASSION BACK!

I remember in the not-too-distant past, one of my best friends was simply 'stuck' in her sadness and despair. I had to think of a way to bring back joy into her life!

With the help of her daughter and a couple of her church friends, we arranged for a picnic at the park. And... to get her back to one of her favorite passions we all knew she had, we told her that she was to bring dessert!

And boy was it the best dessert ever! My friend Ellen made the most delicious Red Velvet chocolate cake with homemade decadent cream cheese filling! And who do you think was smiling ear to ear when she brought it to the picnic table! Uhhh-ummmm!

So.. maybe your friend is into music or crocheting or sports... whatever it may be. Remember their passion and invite them to get 'back in the game'. Trust me, when someone gets their passion back and they're doing what they love, this beyond happy!

YOU TOO CAN BECOME HAPPIER!

When one gives of their time and is generous towards their family and friends, a great blessing is also bestowed on them. When you're trying to make someone happy and get their smile back, you will find yourself being graced with happiness as well.

So here's a big *thank you* to anyone who is out there in the world making people smile. It is a truly admirable thing to do. There is nothing better than to see someone who was 'down in the dumps' find themselves back to smiling again and having joy back into their life.

Friendship isn't about whom you have known the longest... It's about who came and never left your side.

-Unknown

TESTIMONIALS

"I Just Want To Be Happy Again!"

I love your article because it really serves as an important reminder for myself and others dealing with the stresses and worries of everyday life. I too have been sad and what spoke out to me most is being in the present – it's something I struggle with and am working on but just want to thank you for the great reminder.

-- Hannah 9/10/2020

"Giggle, Laugh & Be Silly Once In A while"

Oh boy, do I love this post! I am known as the one to lighten the atmosphere and make people laugh. I feel it is my true gift to help lift up people and spread more light around the world. The downside is I also use humor in stressful situations which means I sometimes laugh inappropriately. I'm glad you brought this topic up because being silly every once in a while is fun as well! Great post!

-- Heather Ritchie

"Feeling Loneliness? 7 Secret Techniques for Dealing with Loneliness"

I'm so glad you commented on the difference between loneliness and being alone. They are NOT the same! I crave my alone time, and like my solitude (esp now that I'm a parent and rarely get any), but I am at a very different place now in my life than when I was younger, constantly surrounded by others, and yet always felt so lonely. Your tips for handling loneliness are spot-on, too.

-- Flossie McCowald

"Six Traits All Happy & Successful People Have PLUS... the Most Secret 7th Trait Revealed"

Thank you for this great article! Resilience and determination are definitely two incredible qualities that you practice (over and over again!) on the way to your dreams. Thank you for the reminder.

-- Celine Harleaux

"How Happy Are You Really?"

I think so many people would benefit from reading this! I love how well put everything was and it was super enlightening. Thanks so much for sharing!

-- Claudia Gebhardt

"The True Value of Friendship & Happiness"

What a great post! Friendship is such a big and important part of our lives. And I love that you point out the qualities of true friendship, because that really does matter. Holding onto relationships that aren't "true friendship" can be unhealthy. Thank you for sharing this!

-- Rose Hahn

"Discovering Your Life's Grand Purpose"

This is one important topic and very nicely explained. Finding life purpose takes time but everyone realizes someday or the other. The crux is living with peace and harmony. Thank you Beth.

-- Jamie Smartkins

"The Power of Forgiveness is a Lifechanger"

So hard to say but so invaluable to do! Great article!

-- Lisa Marie Alioto

"Master the Art of Gratitude With These 15 Tips"

I love your post. I always believe gratitude makes you see the good in every situation, even the bad ones. Thereby helping your mental health and helping you move forward.

-- Olufunke Kolapo

"The Awesome Healing Power of Journaling"

This by far one of the best blog posts I have ever read regarding journaling. I knew journaling had so many benefits, as I used to write a lot, but didn't realize they were so immense. Incredible. Thank you for sharing. This definitely inspires me to write more.

-- Sarah Afshar

"Life Issues – Are You Living or Are You Just Existing?"

Very interesting read. Puts a NEW SPARK in priorities. Especially with what's going on in the world. I really am not in control, my God is and I do my best to do what's in front of me, doing the next right thing and look for the Positive. Beth Elkassih is a BIG MOTIVATOR AND FULL OF INSPIRATION!! Keep up the Great thought provoking, content, Beth!!!

-- Andrea Hyde

"10 Powerful Tips in Overcoming Anxiety Attacks"

Anxiety can be such a debilitating emotion. It's really great that you've given some ideas of different anxieties and how to cope with them. I really like the concept of figuring out your triggers and trying to calm them before they start. Thank you for this.

-- Sasha Lassey

"Finally Take Charge of Your Life & Start Believing in Yourself Again!"

Great blog post! You discussed quite a few important things! I really liked that you mentioned that we don't need others' approval to feel complete!

-- Patty Luu

ABOUT THE AUTHOR

Beth Elkassih is the creator of the professional blog, **"Made You Smile Back"** (https://madeyousmileback.com) which was created in October 2018.

She is also the Author of 'The Power of Unexpected Miracles' which ended up being a Best Seller on **Amazon** in two categories and an International Best Seller in Australia, United Kingdom and Canada in 2019.

In addition, she is the co-author (with **Umair Qureshi**) of three journals - **'The Ultimate Happiness Journal', The Ultimate Journal of Gratitude'** and **'Sacred Love'** -- all available on **Amazon.** Beth is also the proud creator of the growing **Facebook Group, Achieving Happiness**. And just recently, became a certified Happiness Life Coach and Motivational Speaker.

Since 2006, Beth is also a licensed Realtor for the Dallas/Fort Worth Texas Metroplex. Previously Beth attended Truman University in Kirksville MO and Michigan State University in Business Administration studies from 1975-1979. Beth is currently married and has three daughters and lives in Arlington, TX.

"I HAVE WALKED THE WALK AND NOW TALKING THE TALK ABOUT MENTAL HEALTH ISSUES!"

Beth is a survivor of acute post-partum depression. As an avid Mental Health awareness advocate, Beth's vision of **"Made You Smile Back'** is to be an inviting place for those struggling with their own happiness, as a valuable resource in helping them 'get their smile back'. It is her hope to present a platform where all of us can become an active community who make a difference online to others. Find out just what happiness is, gratitude, forgiveness and kindness.

Through her blog, Beth tackles the subjects that need to be discussed which are not being placed in the forefront today. Like chronic depression, sadness, anxiety and even post-partum depression.

In writing this book, **"I Just Want To Be Happy Again"**, and with her platform, **"Made You Smile Back"**, Beth is doing her part in helping remove the stigma of mental health illness.

THANK YOU FOR READING MY BOOK!

Thank you for allowing me to share with you these 14 powerful chapters in order to help you in regaining your happiness, to find yourself again when facing everyday life struggles. If you enjoyed reading these chapters and/or if one resonates with you, I welcome you to visit my blog site ", **'Made You Smile Back"** (www.madeyousmileback.com) to read more related blogs.

This is a no-judgment zone and offers both encouragement and inspiration with thought-provoking content in tackling everyday life difficulties. Please consider sharing with your family and friends.

Reviews are most welcome and also very much appreciated. Plans are in the works for a 2nd Edition of **'The Power of Unexpected Miracles"** entitled **"Unexpected Miracles Happen Everyday"**. Be sure to subscribe to my blog so you can be one of the first to know about the upcoming launch date.

I am also available for motivational speaking and as a Happiness Life Coach. Feel free to reach out to me at beth@madeyousmileback.com

Many Blessings!
Beth Elkassih

Made in the USA
Monee, IL
28 April 2022

95565685R00069